Tales from the Bed

Tales from the Bed

On Living, Dying, and Having It All

A MEMOIR

Jenifer Estess

as told to

Valerie Estess

ATRIA BOOKS

New York London Toronto Sydney

ATRIA BOOKS
1230 Avenue of the Americas
New York, NY 10020

ISBN: 0-7434-7682-4

First Atria Books hardcover edition May 2004

10 9 8 7 6 5 4 3 2 1

ATRIA BOOKS is a trademark of Simon & Schuster, Inc.

Manufactured in the United States of America

For information regarding special discounts for bulk purchases,
please contact Simon & Schuster Special Sales at 1-800-456-6798
or business@simonandschuster.com.

For my sisters, our children, and my mother

Foreword

BY KATIE COURIC

I met Jenifer Estess four years ago at her apartment on West Twelfth Street in New York City. A number of our mutual acquaintances had suggested we meet. They insisted, I resisted. I had lost my husband to colon cancer just two years earlier and I was afraid I was still too fragile to befriend someone with a terminal illness. After being nudged repeatedly, I acquiesced. I headed to Jenifer's that February afternoon, and what can I say? She had me at hello. Call it kismet, call it chemistry, call it fate ... whatever you call it, that was the first day of one of the most meaningful and powerful friendships I've ever experienced. Henry David Thoreau once wrote, "The language of friendship is not words, but meaning. It is intelligence above language." The challenge of expressing all that Jenifer meant to me is humbling and intimidating.

When I first met Jenifer, she was in a wheelchair, ALS just beginning its insidious journey northward. We sat in the living room with Jenifer's two sisters, Valerie and

Meredith, and her dear friend Julianne and talked about this disease called ALS and their search for a cure. In a matter of minutes, I saw not a young woman with a fatal disease but a funny, vibrant, razor-sharp beauty who would quickly become my loyal friend and confidante.

How did I love her? Let me count the ways. Of course there was her amazing courage, grace, and dignity in the face of the most challenging kind of existence and most frightening kind of future. She was the personification of bravery, dealing quietly and matter-of-factly with the indignities of her disease. And she was always so present. When you were with her, you felt that you were the only two people in the world. She was sharp as a tack and had an insatiable appetite for whatever was going on in the world—whether it was a Supreme Court ruling or the latest heartthrob featured on the cover of *People* magazine. Jenifer was generous with her time and her heart. She could have crawled into her proverbial shell and shut people out, but she didn't. She remained so externally focused and completely in the moment.

She was a wonderful listener—a hip and funny Dear Abby, doling out especially good advice in matters of love. She was fiercely loyal. Pity the person who dissed a friend of Jenifer's. She wrote them off, their name never to emanate from her lips again, except in a hilariously catty remark. Most of all, Jenifer was about love. That was her greatest gift. She enveloped you in love and made you feel so special that you sometimes forgot how special she was.

But if loving others was her greatest gift, her sense of

humor had to share top billing on her already remarkable résumé. Jenifer took the elephant in the room and turned it into a circus act. Her remarkable and, yes, deadpan humor (she would have had a field day with my choice of words) got so many of us through a very unfunny situation. I wish I had written down all the "Jeniferisms" I heard over the last four years. "Hi Jenifer, how are you?" "Great, except for this ALS stuff." "Jenifer can I call you right back?" "Sure, but can you give me a few hours? I'm going to run a marathon."

She even proposed a sitcom featuring her beloved nurse Lorna, complete with a theme song sung to the tune of *Three's Company*: "Lorna, please move my leg . . . can you give me a drink?" Jenifer dealt with an outrageous situation by being outrageous herself. And when she could no longer go to the party, the party came to her—up until the end, sitting on her bed, surrounded by legions of friends and the nieces and nephews she adored, Jenifer remained the high priestess of love, laughter, and light.

ALS robbed Jenifer of so much. But through it all, she continued to appreciate the beauty of life even when her ability to live it was so cruelly curtailed. ALS couldn't take away her brilliance, and the one muscle it could not destroy was her heart.

Jenifer cannot be described without mentioning her two sisters, Valerie and Meredith. They so reminded me of the powerful and motivating combination of fear, desperation, and love. I, too, was motivated by those same things when my husband was diagnosed with colon cancer. But while I could cling to a sliver of hope as Jay went through chemotherapy and radiation, there were no such options for Jenifer—no treatment and certainly no cure. Yet, somehow, from this terrible abyss of hopelessness, sprung a thing of beauty: the love, loyalty, and power of this sisterhood.

They say good things come in threes. Pythagoras, the Greek philosopher of the sixth century, called three the perfect number. Man is threefold: body, soul, and spirit. The world consists of earth, sea, and air. And in Greek mythology there are three fates, three furies, and three graces. These three sisters should be added to that list. I will always think of them as a perfect triangle, providing each other with strong, steady, unconditional support. Take one away, and all that is left is a plain, straight line. Jenifer was taken away, but she'll forever be the apex of that triangle, the pinnacle of courage and grace to which we can all aspire.

Jenifer and her sisters had a favorite expression. Whenever anything seemed unattainable, like being asked out by a ridiculously handsome guy, they'd say with an air of bemused resignation, "Hopes!" But Jenifer's life raised ours, and thanks to the Estess sisters, finding a cure for ALS is no longer unattainable.

My friend Jenifer Estess made everything seem possible. While it now may not be possible to call her, to see her, to laugh with her, it is still possible to love her. I do and always will.

Tales from the Bed

Chapter One

MARCH 17, 1997, was a very windy day in New York City. Walking up Amsterdam Avenue to the gym that morning, I wanted to turn around and go home. The old me would have. My apartment was dark and inviting, my bed was warm, and the gym would be there tomorrow. But then I thought of the Muffin Shop, which was opening in an hour. If I worked out for an hour, I could stop by on the way home for a muffin and coffee to go. One of the great pleasures for me was sitting at my new kitchen table with my muffin and coffee, planning the day. I had a big day ahead of me, so I kept going.

I'd been listening to Annie Lennox a lot on my Walkman. She was instrumental in some of the recent changes for the better I'd made in my life. Annie didn't sing—she spoke to me. "Please get your butt on the treadmill, Jenifer," she said. I always loved that English accent. *Right-ee-o, Annie.*

After six months, I had worked up to thirty minutes of

1

running at 5.0 on the treadmill. Then I'd stretch and do a hundred, make that seventy sit-ups on the mat. I looked around the gym for my friend Billy Baldwin, who did sit-ups with me, but he wasn't there. The sit-ups were harder that morning, which was strange because I had a pretty strong stomach. I had to stop a few times. A handsome trainer walking by asked if I was okay. I said that I certainly thought so. He winked at me and kept going. *Sixty-seven . . . sixty-eight . . . Talk to me, Annie.* I dripped sweat. Hard-core athletes dripped sweat like this. I thought I was getting into some kind of shape. My sister Valerie would be proud.

Back at home I sat at my new table, feeling its smooth, sturdy contours. It had been a major purchase for me, the perfect Williams-Sonoma starter for a woman on the verge. I had my whole table in front of me, my blueberry muffin in hand, and a boy in my eyes. I hadn't met the boy yet. That would be happening tonight at Raoul's, a popular restaurant in Soho. My friends Martha and Merrill were going to spy on my date and me from another table. If it felt right, I'd give Martha the high sign, and the four of us would go dancing from there. Dating was something I didn't do much of in my twenties. I think people were a little worried about me. I kept saying I wasn't ready, I wasn't ready. Then, when I realized I'd never be ready, I told my friends to fix me up, and suddenly there was an all-points bulletin out for an eligible guy for me. On some level, I still thought that blind dates were for losers, but I was learning to keep my eye on the prize. What I wanted most was to love someone and to have children. Maybe tonight was a step in that direction. It probably wasn't going to be *West Side Story,* but maybe it would be. *Could be . . .*

I sipped my coffee, forever my drink of choice. It was all about this kind of loving self-discipline: one muffin at a time, not two, eaten like a human being sitting at my gorgeous new table, not out of the bag on the run. Most of my friends were married and having babies or inviting me to showers or lamenting not getting married. I was starting to bask in self-reliance—I was working hard, step-by-step, to make my dream life a reality. My design for living was simple: I drew on the lessons of my girlhood. I was taking good care of my body. I was making a safe, comfortable home for myself. I was on a roll workwise. The ideas came fast and furious: *Maybe for my next birthday I'd register at Bloomingdale's. Why should I have to wait for a fiancé to get a couch?*

"Oofah," I said, pushing back from the breakfast table. I was really late for work. I suddenly remembered the loofah brush and lavender soaps I'd picked up from Crabtree & Evelyn for my date. They were still in a shopping bag on the floor in my closet. When I bent down to get it, I got stuck in a crouch. As I got to my feet, and it took a minute, my burgundy silk shirt hanging from above fell into the Crabtree bag. Surely that was a sign. I'd do the burgundy silk shirt tonight, with my black jeans, and the brown suede jacket . . . or my black Donna Karan coat. The coat was dressier, a three-quarter length, and gorgeous. *Keep him guessing with the combination of*

*dressy on the outside and totally casual-comfortable under-
neath.*

Running for the shower, I waved to my new
Fiestaware plates stacked on the kitchen counter. I hadn't
cooked a meal in years, but I would cook soon. I'd start
with something simple—a pasta, maybe? Then came my
really weird shower experience. As I unwrapped my
loofah and my bathroom filled with steam, I imagined
my date—rumored to be very handsome—watching me
walk oh so elegantly through the steam toward the shower. Like those showgirls through dry ice in Las Vegas. But
that wasn't even the weird part. Suddenly I felt oh . . . so
. . . bogged down, as if I were wearing a wet wool blanket. I went into slow-motion showering, loo . . . fah . . .
ing, and drying off. The towel was heavy, too, a second
wet wool blanket. Was there such a thing as working out
too much?

I blow-dried my hair in a hurry, never a problem. My
hair was my calling card—thick chocolate chunks of excellence, very Marlo Thomas in *That Girl*. My hair had gotten
me through a lot in life. When I was posing for my head
shot in second grade, I brushed my hair carefully around
my slightly chubby face. I knew instinctively how to use my
hair to create illusions of lankiness and great beauty. For as
long as I could remember, I led with my hair.

As I ran down Columbus Avenue to catch a cab, I had
my own *That Girl* moment. I saw my whole life coming
toward me: I saw him and them, a husband and children,
as true possibilities. I saw my sisters Valerie and Meredith

walking in stride with great purpose. There I was between them, walking confidently. I looked pretty good. *Diamonds, daisies, Broadway*—wow. The wind really kicked up. It was so strong it pushed me backward. I sweated and slowed down on the sidewalk just as I had in the shower. I tried to fight the wind. I tried accelerating on the human highway of tourists walking to the St. Patrick's Day Parade, but there was nothing in my tank. I was alone in a sea of Kelly green. I wanted to tell everyone it was a great day for the Irish—and me, too—but they just kept passing me. I wanted them to know I was going to Raoul's that night. I wanted to tell them that I was lucky, and that I had my whole life ahead of me. Did I mention the wind? It was really blowing. It had a personality now—it wanted me dead.

I felt instant relief at the office with my feet up on the desk. My office was absolutely gorgeous, a dramatic departure from the alternative spaces I'd worked in as an off-Broadway theater producer. It was twenty marble-appointed floors up in a luxury midtown high-rise with great air-conditioning and a view of Central Park— salary *so* not commensurate. The job itself was a little disappointing. I was doing public relations, which I didn't care for, but in the end my office was the perfect front. Behind closed doors, twenty floors above Central Park, Valerie, Meredith, and I were planning a creative coup. Since high school, my sisters and I had had the idea of starting our own movie studio, and I was finally putting that plan into action. After years of hard work, Valerie,

Meredith, and I were finally pursuing our best laid plans of childhood. It had taken us a while, but I felt sure that our hard work was about to pay off.

Meredith walked into my office for one of our top-secret working lunches just as my boss, smiling and totally unsuspecting, was walking out. My boss was a nice enough person. I knew one day she'd forgive me for the empire I was about to create. From across the desk, I watched Meredith lean in to her lunch, a tuna sandwich from Mangia, one of the best places in the city for tuna.

This was the moment I'd lived for, relaxing with my little sister over perfect tuna before an afternoon's worth of hard work. I reached for my sandwich feeling proud not only of Meredith but of my evolving perspective on food. I ate when I was hungry, that was all. I kicked my legs back up on the desk and started writing a few overdue checks.

"I see your legs," Meredith said.

"Who doesn't?" I said.

"No, seriously," she said, and she was right. The twitches in my legs that Valerie, Meredith, and I had seen occasionally over the last few months were going wild. My thigh muscles moved like snakes under my black slacks. They undulated and piled up on one another. I agreed it was bizarre. Meredith put down her sandwich. She saw twitches in my arms, too.

"I don't like it," she said. It was scary when Meredith weighed in. My little sister always meant what she said.

"Maybe I should see a doctor," I said.

"Like now," Meredith said, but I wanted to work. After lunch Meredith and I talked about a movie treatment that Valerie had written. I still felt the twitches in my legs, but I didn't want to look down at them. I wanted to look anywhere else. I wanted to look at my Fiesta plates and start the day over. *Don't look down.* I wanted to look out of my window at the thousand Kelly green dots of people marching, gliding, walking, running, pushing, strolling, kissing through Central Park. *Keep working.* I wanted to look at Meredith like this forever, an amazing woman in the prime of her life. Just like me.

"Look down." My heart talks, I listen. The muscles of my legs and arms were rolling like the sea. As usual, my heart knew what my head would learn. Against the backdrop of my picture window, against the eagle's view of New York, my city, the impossible truth was announced: Something was seriously wrong with me.

The doctors invited me to a square dance. My first partner was my internist. I called him Undershorts. Undershorts was so tiny he could have fit under my exam gown. When I pulled up my gown to show him my twitches, he blushed and looked away. Then he climbed up onto a ladder and examined my ears, eyes, and throat. Undershorts didn't find anything wrong, so he swung me out to my second partner, Dr. Hainline, a sports neurologist at the Hospital for Joint Diseases. I bowed to my partner.

"Benign fasciculations," pronounced a busy Dr.

Hainline, whose dance card was full. He said *fascicula-tions* was the clinical term for the muscle twitches I'd been experiencing. Apparently, my fasciculations had resulted from an unremarkable misfiring of nerve cells. I was fine. Good to go. That deserved a do-si-do.

That next week, I had trouble walking up the stairs when I was with my friend Nicole at the theater. "You didn't say anything about stairs," said Dr. Hainline, dur-ing my second visit to his office, and he danced to the left. "I'm going to run one test," he said, "but I know it'll come out negative." Negative was positive, I remembered from my days watching *Medical Center.*

What's a square dance without a good psychiatrist? After I booked my appointment for the test, I placed an emergency call to my shrink, Karen. She reminded me of Sally Field. I loved Karen, I really did. She had been one of my clear-thinking, commonsense beacons in the last couple of years, mentoring me item by item down the having-it-all checklist: weight loss (check), dating (check), landing a better-paying job (half-a-check). The Zoloft didn't hurt, either.

When I rolled up my sleeve to show her my arm mus-cles moving, Karen fidgeted, she crossed and uncrossed her legs—she was all over the dance floor. My common-sense beacon was having a neurotic break with reality. Our repartee, which had always been verbal and jokey, filled up with more pauses than a Pinter play.

"Karen," I said.

"Jenifer," she said.

I placed my palms on the Abercrombie & Fitch jeans that she had helped me fit into. Karen was a medical doctor. I wondered, *Didn't she want to mosey on over and examine me?*

"The twitching is getting really bad," I said.

"The twitching . . . ," she said.

"You remember . . . the twitching." Was this an echo chamber? "The neurologist thinks it's all in my head," I said.

"Do *you* think it's all in your head?" Karen asked. That was all I could stand. I swung my partner and let go, quite frankly. For all I know, Karen's still reeling down Central Park West.

On March 26, I went for my EMG, the one test that Dr. Hainline had said would show nothing. The EMG measures how well your nerves talk to your muscles. I wasn't sure what that had to do with me. The EMG room was small and filthy, with a big computer. My mother sat next to me in a folding chair. Valerie was next to me on the exam table, as a tall woman taped cold foil discs all over my body, turned to the computer keyboard, and tap-tap-tapped with her back to us for about ten minutes. The tall woman rose, wished me luck, and left the room. Then a very pregnant radiologist came in. She had a thick Russian accent. My ancestors were Russian, or at least I thought they were.

"Weren't our ancestors Russian?" I asked my mother, swinging my legs off the side of the table.

"Who knows? Who cares?" she said. My mother

wasn't exactly the family historian. Our family didn't really have a historian.

The pregnant radiologist asked me to lie down for the second part of the test. She stuck long, sharp needles into different muscles in my arms, legs, and torso. It hurt a little. Each time she stuck me, the computer recorded data. After about fifty sticks, she rose. "Please wait," she said, pausing at the doorway and exiting stage right. People came and went so quickly here.

Minutes passed. Fifteen minutes. Valerie was losing her temper. She looked down the hall and saw a huddle of white coats. The huddle broke and a third doctor came in. With a Russian accent so thick you could cut it with a scythe—radiology must have been all the rage in Moscow—he introduced himself as the director of the department. He asked me if I had taken any prescription drugs lately. There was the Zoloft and an occasional Advil. He asked me if I used cocaine. I was always too scared to try it. The doctor scratched his five-o'clock shadow. He inserted two last needles, one into my neck and one into my tongue. That hurt a lot. I saw my mother grab Valerie's arm. The doctor wrote on a clipboard for a long time. Then he wheeled around in his chair to face us.

"Well, there *is* something," he said. It was the moment of truth in a made-for-TV movie. I went numb. As for the earth, it shifted 180 degrees. "I'd say it's fifty-fifty."

"*What's* fifty-fifty?" I asked.

The director shrugged and sent us downstairs to Dr. Hainline, who had prescribed the EMG, the one test that was going to come back negative. We sat for hours waiting for Hainline. For kicks, nothing beats a neurologist's waiting room, especially after a preliminary diagnosis of *fifty-fifty*. A middle-aged couple, the man's head wrapped in yellowed gauze, held each other and wept. A limping child hurtled scarily toward a pile of toys. A woman with an evangelist's stare looked only at the ceiling. A receptionist finally appeared.

"I must say I'm surprised by the results of your EMG," Dr. Hainline said. He buried his head in my manila file. "You seem to have some kind of motor neuron disease."

"What the hell is a motor neuron disease?" Valerie asked.

When I heard *motor,* I immediately thought of going somewhere, of getting up and running out, and never stopping. I thought of movement. The phrase itself—*motor neuron disease*—didn't conjure up anything specific. But I knew it was bad. Instinct ordered me to leave my body and supervise from above. My spirit hovered over the scene, trying to make sense of a new phrase—and what I sensed was going to be a whole new life.

"Will I be able to walk?" I asked.

"We'll keep an eye on that," he said. Dr. Hainline spoke in tongues, ancient doctors' tongues.

"Is it a virus?" Valerie asked.

"No one knows for sure," he said.

11

"Will I be able to play tennis?" I asked.

"I've been at it for thirty years and I still can't play," he said, laughing and blushing. I pictured Valerie smashing a ball down Dr. Hainline's throat, but she and I pressed on responsibly with our twenty questions. So far, motor neuron disease hadn't qualified as animal, vegetable, or mineral. We looked for answers, even grains of answers.

"Will this situation clear up? Does it come and go?" Valerie asked.

"Need a more definitive diagnosis first," said the doctor.

"I've been working out a lot lately, maybe too much," I offered.

"Agreed!" declared my mother, jumping in bravely. "If I may . . . Dr. Hainline . . . what my daughter does to her body at that gym is dangerous, with the weights and the running and the going and the coming. It's too much for any one human—too much."

"Hmmm," said Hainline, closing my file, blushing crimson.

"Can you give us anything to hang our hats on?" Valerie asked.

"I can give you a wonderful referral," said Dr. Hainline, heading for the door. "Up at Columbia," Hainline said. "He's a giant in the field." I pictured the Jolly Green Giant on a box of frozen baby peas. I ate a lot of those peas when I was a girl. I liked the butter sauce.

I had a motor neuron disease and a giant at Columbia University was going to tell me what that meant. Maybe he could take it away. I felt my arms and legs disappearing right then and there. *I must have a fast-moving case,* I thought. Dr. Hainline's receptionist handed me a card with the giant's phone number on it, and my mother, Valerie, and I left the hospital.

It was a black-and-blue night in New York. I was changed from before. I was a different woman hailing a taxi. My mother dropped us off at Valerie's house in Greenwich Village. Valerie, Scott, and their baby boy, Willis, lived in an ancient brownstone on Jones Street, a quiet street. Their house was my haven. After work, I loved hopping in a cab and going down to see them. Willis was my little blond duck. The house always smelled so good, like Valerie's chicken or her pasta cooking. There was always a place set for me. That night I wanted to stay and never leave.

We didn't do much crying or talking that night. Everyone just got busy. Scott set up my foldout cot in the living room. Valerie asked what we thought of spaghetti and a salad. Willis ran around in his diaper. Once, when he was eight months old, Willis and I pressed our foreheads together and laughed like no one had ever heard. We knew how to reach each other. That night, after Valerie and Scott had gone downstairs to bed, Willis and I started our sleepover. We were the night birds of the family. I opened a box of animal crackers, and we sat on the cot changing channels and laughing at everyone until midnight. We settled on a Hercules serial dubbed in Spanish, and Willis fell asleep in my arms. As I held him, I watched Hercules picking people up, throwing them down, and carrying them to safety. Maybe Spanish Hercules would save me. But in all likelihood, that job was going to be mine.

In April, after that horrible March madness, I finally had my appointment with the giant in the field, Dr. Lewis P. Rowland, the director of the Neurological Institute of New York at Columbia University. Dr. Rowland was a happier version of my grandfather George, a kind, handsome, incredibly successful Chevrolet dealer from the Bronx, who never smiled. Dr. Rowland was old-school all the way, right down to the threadbare Oriental in his book-lined office and his wardrobe of bow ties. In fact, Dr. Rowland had been around long enough to have actually attended the Old School.

On the day of my appointment, I asked Meredith and Valerie to "answer phones at my office," code for moving our fledgling movie studio to the next planning stages. When they found it impossible to concentrate, my sisters went to St. Patrick's Cathedral and prayed. I'd asked my mother and oldest sister, Alison, to take me to Dr. Rowland's office at the Neurological Institute. The institute was a huge brick fortress that looked like a prison. I got the feeling that you checked in to a place like the institute, but you didn't check out.

"What brings you here, Miss Estess?" asked Dr. Rowland as I approached his mahogany desk the size of a ship. Maybe I left my legs in the cab. I couldn't feel them.

"I have a motor neuron disease," I said. I was Dorothy facing the Wizard.

"You don't have motor neuron disease," Dr. Rowland boomed, my file from Dr. Hainline sitting closed on his desk. Dr. Rowland's friends called him Bud.

"Oh my God, I don't?" I said.

"No, no. You don't have motor neuron disease," he said again.

Oh, Bud. I swooned. The other doctors were such amateurs. Just like that, Dr. Rowland commuted my sentence. They didn't call this guy the giant for nothing. My mother wept for joy. Alison ran out to call Valerie and Meredith. I was going to be okay. That meant I'd live to dance at my mother's weddings.

Then Dr. Rowland opened my file from Dr. Hainline, for the first time, I guess. As he reviewed the file, his face screwed up into a ghastly seriousness. *Bud, you've changed.* "Step out, please," he said to my mother, ushering her out of the office in a hurry. So much for peas in butter sauce; color drained out of the world.

"I'm sorry, Miss Estess. You'll forgive me," he said gravely as he and I sat alone. "I hadn't seen the results of your EMG or your spinal tap," Dr. Rowland said. "I saw you . . . and I spoke out of turn. I've not done that before. Of course, I'll want to run my own tests."

Dr. Rowland gave me a neurological exam right there in his office. He followed my eyes with a flashlight. He hit my knees with a giant rubber hammer. He dragged a foot-long Q-Tip across the soles of my feet. For diagnosing motor neuron disease, the giant in the field used clown props.

"May I ask you to sit on the floor, Miss Estess, and then stand up?" *Tumbling?* All these weird tests, these Rube Goldberg variations, seemed so unscientific. But I was determined to win Bud over. If this was the extra-credit test, I felt sure I could ace it, charm him, and change his mind back again to *you don't have motor neuron disease.* After all, I could be very persuasive. I ran my fingers through my hair and settled onto Bud's Oriental like a lotus flower. I was great. I was graceful. I made good eye contact. Then I tried to stand up. I gave it my all—I used my arms and legs, and the stomach muscles I'd worked on at the gym—but I couldn't get off the floor. Dr. Rowland extended his hand, helped me up to a chair, and kneeled before me.

"You probably have ALS, Jenifer," he said, resting his hand on my knee. "Let's take a walk." Dr. Rowland and I walked arm in arm down an endless beige hallway. He told me that ALS was amyotrophic lateral sclerosis, a neuromuscular disease that destroys cells in the brain and spine called motor neurons. Without motor neurons, the brain can't tell the muscles what to do. Without directions from the brain, muscles can't function. Without muscles, a person can't walk, speak, swallow, breathe. . . . It was all getting a little confusing.

"Will I be able to have children?" I asked.

"You can have them," he said. "I just don't know if you'll be able to keep up with them." I started crying.

"We will have no tears," Bud said. He put his arm

around me. I think Dr. Rowland assumed that because I'd walked in to his office that afternoon young, confident, and self-possessed I was also healthy. Poor Bud.

The only thing I remember after the beige hallway was collapsing into Valerie's arms. She held me like a mother while I made sounds I didn't recognize. They were animal sounds, sounds from nature, unplanned sounds. *This is what a dying woman sounds like.* Then Meredith moved in close and we three huddled as one. Silently, Valerie, Meredith, and I renewed a sacred girlhood pact: *Nothing, no one will stop us.* Over the next months, I would come to reject conventional wisdom, the books and TV shows advising me to let go as I died. For my sisters and me, dying, as living, wasn't about letting go. Holding on to each other was what we knew. Holding on like this and reaching.

Dr. Rowland admitted to making a terrible mistake that day, one that I forgave. But as I soon learned, ALS was much less forgiving. The Yankee baseball legend Lou Gehrig died from it, and so did every single one of the hundreds of thousands of other people who got it. No one survived. There was no medicine for ALS, and nothing Dr. Rowland could give me would slow it down or stop it. I was thirty-five years old. My cells were dying. I was dying. Dr. Rowland didn't say that exactly—he gave that job to his nurse and a bunch of pamphlets.

But for some weird reason, Dr. Rowland kept hanging

around me after that first day. As I fought for my life, he taught me to buck up and be strong. He listened to me. He had my back. From that day on, Bud Rowland became the father I never had. I'm still trying to make him proud.

Chapter Two

MY REAL FATHER'S NAME was Gene, ironic given that a gene on chromosome 21 is responsible for one form of ALS. I didn't have that form of ALS per se, but scientists believe that I and others with so-called sporadic ALS are genetically predisposed to it. In other words, my DNA, or the genetic blueprint I was born with, made me a prime candidate for the disease.

I don't remember much about my father, but in his case a little goes a long way. Gene Estess grew up the favorite child of Adolph and Lillian Estess, a Jewish couple who lived in a pretty house on the banks of the Mississippi River, in Rock Island, Illinois, deep in Mark Twain country. My father was a shapely man, not like a farmer or a machinist, the kind of guys you saw around Rock Island. He was large and curvaceous. I thought he was handsome in his own special way. "Your father is *great*-looking," my mother always said, loud enough for him to hear. I took her word for it. My mother was a major tastemaker of her time.

My father wore a toupee. There's no question he would have looked better bald, but he opted instead for the three inches of cheesecloth. My father's toupee was a real presence in our house. It was a regular member of the family, with its jet-black hair, double-stick adhesive strips, and its own personal Styrofoam stand in the shape of a human head. Eventually my father's toupee came to symbolize much more to our family—cover-ups. Gene Estess was the Richard Nixon of fathers. I loved him; I looked up to him; I was onto him. My sister Valerie said I always knew things first. I suspected from a very early age that my father was an unfaithful person.

One of my father's outstanding features was his sense of entitlement. Lore has it that as a sophomore visiting home from college, Gene marched into the Star Restaurant, a Rock Island burger joint, and demanded an immediate change in the menu. He wanted a beef tenderloin sandwich added to it. Sliced beef tenderloin had become my father's favorite sandwich back East at the University of Pennsylvania, and he expected Rock Island to get with the program. My grandpa Adolph made a call to the owner of the Star and it was done. A beef tenderloin sandwich became the first menu addition in the history of the place. Thanks to my dad, you could now order a hamburger, a cheeseburger, or a beef tenderloin sandwich there. My father was a big man with big appetites. He expected them filled.

In 1957, at the age of twenty, Gene had an appetite for my mother, Marilyn. He fell in love with her at a college mixer. I knew he fell in love because I found his old letters to her in my grandma's attic. Those letters don't lie. My mother said my father was "sick drunk" the night they met. From there, her account of their courtship gets murky.

"Was it love at first sight, Mommy?" I asked over coffee.

"How should I know? He was passed out and vomiting," she said. My mother and I talked over coffee a lot. I was her Rock Island confidante. As she drank black coffee and painted complicated word pictures, I looked at her and listened, captivated, as if I were watching a movie. My mother, who was a master at using her imagination to transport herself to better places, told me many secrets over coffee. She told me that our family was special. We were spectacular, she confided, and gifted. "You'll see," she said. "You'll see." I learned the power of the imagination from my mother. From our time together, I learned to love listening. I found I was good at it. I was good at listening, probing, and advising.

"But, Mommy," I persisted, "you had so many boyfriends. There was that football player from Stamford—"

"*Stanford,*" she said, dragging deeply on her Salem cigarette.

"And that nice boy from Dartmouth," I said.

"Your father was the right person at the right time," she said, exhaling.

My parents got engaged two months after they met, then married lavishly at The Plaza hotel in New York. I thought they made a handsome couple. In fact, I still measure the elegance of a wedding by my parents' black-and-white photo album, a fairy-tale scrapbook that I memorized as a girl.

My mother was without a doubt the most beautiful woman in Rock Island, the Bronx (where she was born), and maybe the world. I'm talking drop-dead gorgeous. She was Faye Dunaway before there was a Faye Dunaway. I idolized her face and perfect figure, her clothes, and her sense of style, all of which she trucked out to Rock Island dutifully, right after the wedding. It's safe to say that my mother's many gifts, her deep intelligence and artist's eye, were lost on greater Rock Island. She roamed the cornfields dressed in Pucci, size 0. I felt protective of her. Some days, when I sensed that my mother was in danger and needed my protection, I would make myself sick and stay home from nursery school. I sensed danger as a girl. I had a built-in radar for it.

No house in Rock Island ended up being quite right for my parents, so they built their own Camelot, on a hill. My mother put everything she had into designing our new house, the oddest, most modern structure Rock Island had ever seen. I was proud when the local newspaper came over to interview my mother about her "architectural influences." That was my mother—she could have written her own ticket as an architect, a clothing designer, an artist, a lawyer, anything. I think she really wanted to be an actress.

My mother taught me that there are no small parts, only small actors. She had one line in her senior play at Skidmore College. Her job was to stand on a wooden log and say, "He went thataway." On opening night, as my mother delivered the line, her log began to roll stage right. He went thataway, all right, and so did my mother. She rolled right off the stage. It brought the house down. That was the power of one line, she said, delivered with *umph* to the back of the house. My mother seemed like a happier person when she talked about theater.

With all that talent and nowhere to put it, my mother ended up doing what she claimed every other woman of her generation did at the time—she got pregnant. The first in her family to graduate from college, my mother received her diploma from Skidmore while carrying her first baby, my sister Alison, in a sling. Then in the next six years, at Moline Hospital near Rock Island, she had the rest of us: Valerie, Jenifer, Meredith, and Noah—four girls and a boy. Sometimes I think my mother endured the girls just so she could have a son.

"Don't be ridiculous," she always said. "There's nothing like a girl."

Noah was born sick with a serious form of epilepsy that kept him and my mother in a Chicago hospital for the first year of his life. Doctors couldn't figure out how to control my brother's grand mal seizures, which were happening at the crazy rate of several per hour. I went to

Chicago once to see him. I wandered off to where I shouldn't have been and saw my brother's swaddled silhouette through the darkened window of a room filled with sick babies. He bent in half like a billfold, opening and closing, over and over, uncontrollably. What the hell was happening, and why weren't the doctors doing anything to help my brother? It doesn't take a brain surgeon to connect the dots. My family had its neurological issues: Noah's epilepsy, which would take him years to get under control; my grandfather George's debilitating depression; assorted migraine and anxiety disorders; my ALS. Brainwise, rather than drawing from a gene pool, my family drew from a gene cesspool.

Once my mother had five children, she had to figure out what to do with us. We definitely looked good. She sent for outfits from New York by the exclusive children's designer Florence Eisman and dressed us up. I loved my white gloves and my pretty patent-leather purse to match. Noah wore knickers, scalloped collars, and saddle shoes, just like John-John Kennedy. He was cute like John. Lending new meaning to the phrase *all dressed up and nowhere to go,* my sisters, brother, and I milled about Rock Island, visiting local wildlife amusements like Fedge-a-very Park, where a bored family of goats stood in a pen while we ruined our dresses with ketchup and ice cream. One of my favorite Polaroids is of my mother looking devastatingly gorgeous at Fedge-a-very Park, despite the five of us hanging on her like monkeys.

We children spent most of our time in Rock Island with our baby-sitter, Kaka. Her name was Kathleen, but baby Alison couldn't say that. *Ka . . . Ka,* Alison said. And it stuck. My Kaka smelled really good, like apples and honey. She used to make brownies—if anyone sold them now she'd be very wealthy, but the recipe is lost. The brownies would come out of the oven, and as Kaka stood there with a spatula in her hand, my sisters and I would eat them hot, right out of the pan.

My parents traveled to New York a lot in those years. At least they told us they were going to New York. I had a feeling they were really just dropping us off at Kaka's house and going back home for a rest. Sometimes my sisters and I lived at Kaka's little saltbox for weeks at a time. Kaka had long, long hair the color of hay that she wore up in a perfect bun. Her skin was soft and felt like peach fuzz when she held me to her. Late at night, after she tucked Meredith and me into our beds, I'd sneak into the hall outside her bathroom and watch her put her teeth in a glass. I could never tell how old she was. Kaka was one of the last surviving pioneers, strong as an ox—and so resourceful. From the grapes in her backyard she made jelly. From the flour in her kitchen she made golden crust for pies. From the yarn in her wicker basket, she knitted fisherman sweaters for my dollies.

"I feel exhausted just watching you," my mother said to Kaka, during a rare appearance in Kaka's kitchen. At night, my sisters and I watched TV with Kaka and her husband, Ed, a retired Navy man and machinist for

International Harvester. I think they considered us their children. Ed sat with Valerie in his remote control recliner. Kaka rocked in her chair, sewing and knitting. I was on the floor, my head on my hands, as close as I could get to the huge black-and-white set. I loved television deeply. As an emotional, slightly chubby girl of five, I flung myself into the dramas of the small screen. I watched them all, *Ed Sullivan, The Wonderful World of Disney,* anything Hayley Mills. Once when Ed hooted at a barmaid on *Bonanza* who had just had her heart broken by a cowboy, I told him, "You leave me alone—and you leave that lady alone, too," and I stomped out of the room. Kaka always got a kick out of that line. She quoted it until her death. Ed just laughed at me. But he'd see soon enough. They'd all see. I was secretly grooming myself to be *someone,* a personality, a star—and big, big, big. The fact that I could eat a box of Twinkies at one sitting didn't exactly hurt my chances.

When I was six and my mother told me that we were leaving Rock Island to live in New York, I told her I supported that. "I love you, Mommy," I said, and I went right to my room to pack. She told me that through family connections, she'd helped land my father a job as an account executive with Gray Advertising. My mother felt that my father could grow in advertising. The seven of us would live temporarily with her parents, my grandma and grandpa Rosenberg, in their spacious new house in Harrison, an affluent suburb north of Manhattan. Once in Harrison, we'd find a special house of our own, she promised me, a bigger, better Camelot.

"Will I have my own room?" I asked.

"And then some," my mother said. "And then some."

I was going to miss Kaka and the simple pleasures—the smell of the vinyl seats of her creaky old Corvair on a hot day, her singing "Peace in the Valley" to me as we fished together for catfish in the Mississippi, and the brownies. I was too young for nostalgia, though, and ready for adventure, so I put my dolls and their sweaters in a suitcase and said good-bye. We packed the station wagon, plugged our portable TV in to the lighter socket, and drove away. After I toasted my future with one last frosty mug at the A&W Drive-In, as night fell, my family merged with the open road. One by one, my sisters and brother fell asleep. I sat in the way-backseat, glued to the TV. It was sending me private black-and-white messages, comforting messages, exciting ones. The broken horizontal lines, the muted audio, the grainy faces of the world's biggest stars—it was all a secret code telling me I was about to enter a new world. As my father drove, the messages came through the television, through the night, through Illinois, Ohio, Pennsylvania, and New Jersey. And they were all good.

Chapter Three

"GO DEEP." Valerie gripped the football in her left hand as Meredith and I ran out across the huge front lawn of our new house, Trilarch, named by its previous owners for the clutch of three unremarkable larch trees that welcomed visitors to the three-acre property. Trilarch was a lavish expanse for Harrison, New York, and it was all ours, sort of.

"This one's for . . . Jenifer." Valerie called my number and threw long to within inches of my chubby, outstretched fingers. Desperate to make contact with the ball, I went horizontal and hit the ground hard. The pass was incomplete. I cried into my hair and the dirt. People made fun of my crying. They compared me to the famous actress Sarah Bernhardt, except, they said, I was more like Sarah *Heartburn*.

"Uh-oh, here comes Coach," Meredith said. Meredith had nothing to worry about. She had already caught three bombs, the long throws that Valerie used to test our running and catching skills.

"What seems to be the problem?" Valerie asked, standing over me on the ground. My sister Valerie was one scary eleven-year-old. She looked like a tree with her stringy brown hair for branches and a pretty scowl. Valerie told me to stop crying, but that wasn't happening. I'd been very honest with her: I didn't like football or baseball or any of the other sports she made us play. I liked ice-skating. At least there were outfits and a snack bar, and my legs looked great in those nude opaque tights—

"Get up and do it again," said Valerie. Life with Valerie was well defined. She was the Coach. Meredith and I were her players. We did as she said.

"What about Meredith?" I asked.

"Did Meredith catch a bomb?" Valerie was up in my face.

"Yes," I said.

"Did *you* catch a bomb?" she asked.

"No, Coach, I didn't catch a bomb," I said, hanging my head.

"Don't hang your head," she barked. "Ever." I looked to the sky. My tears fell on the ground.

"Do you want to achieve your personal best on the field, or do you want to cry in your room?"

"Is that a rhetorical question?" I asked.

Valerie wasn't amused. She took Meredith's and my education very seriously. After school and before dinner, Valerie made our every minute count. After supervising our sports, she marched us over to our playhouse in the backyard. Our playhouse was nicer than some people's real houses. It was an FAO Schwarz exclusive—a sturdy cabin with a white picket fence and its own lookout tower, where I watched for enemies. Valerie would change the personality of the playhouse periodically to suit her interests. The first year, our playhouse was the Monkees Fan Club of Harrison. Valerie appointed herself president and plastered pictures from *Tiger Beat* of Micky Dolenz, her favorite Monkee, all over the walls. My job, as I saw it, was to love the Monkees' lead singer, Davy Jones, with my whole heart forever. My job, as Valerie saw it, was to keep the clubhouse clean at all times. Meredith and I were expected to wait on Valerie's friends when they came over for Monkees meetings. We served the older girls snacks that we ran over from our real house.

The second year, Valerie turned our playhouse into the Science Lab. She made Meredith and me watch while she dissected grasshoppers and butterflies with a scalpel. "Don't you find this fascinating?" she asked, slicing into the pale white stomach of a frog.

"I do," said Meredith. Yeah, sure she did.

"I gotta be honest, Valerie. This just isn't me," I said.

"We appreciate your honesty," said Valerie, pulling back the frog's belly to reveal a gut filled with surprisingly vivid reds and blues. "But the world isn't about you, Jenifer."

Valerie educated Meredith and me across disciplines. She taught us science, sports, the latest music. She taught us survival techniques on the nature trail, an overgrown part of our property. I'd be lying if I said that I loved the daily lessons. But basic training wasn't meant to be fun or easy. Basic training was something you hated being in the throes of and appreciated later on. I paid my dues on the field every day. I tried my best, listening and learning until dinner was over. Then it was my turn. When Valerie finally retired to her room for homework, I closed the door to my own room and warmed up to Frank Sinatra. I loved Frank. If my father and I shared anything, it was our deep admiration for Sinatra. I felt cool liking the same singer as my father.

Nighttime was my time. In the privacy of my bedroom I worked on improvised monologues in my vanity mirror. I transformed myself into Cher and Barbra Streisand. I listened to my parents' Judy Garland records until my close-and-play gave out. Okay, maybe I was a gay man trapped in the body of a nine-year-old girl, but who cared? I was too busy performing, working, getting out the kinks—life in the spotlight of the moon was my destiny. And there was no way I was going to face my destiny without Meredith, my little football star. That was the picking order—Valerie picked mostly on me, I picked on Meredith.

"And five, six, seven, eight . . . ," I said, tapping out time. Whenever I wanted, I dragged Meredith through the halls of Trilarch by her beautiful black hair and locked her in my room. I hadn't raised a fool—Meredith knew she'd have to dance her way out.

"Relax the feet," I said from my vanity table, as Meredith attempted a stiff soft-shoe that fell way short. I told her I'd be over to demonstrate the proper technique the moment my nails dried. My new nails were real beauties—pink, frosted, and fake—a new arrival at Polk's, Harrison's superior five-and-dime store. Jumping beans, sewing kits, the largest conceivable selection of fake nails and eyelashes—these were Polk's specialties, and I was a preferred customer. The smell of the greasepaint was one thing—the glue fumes from my new Sally Hansens were a pure shot of energy. I jumped up from my vanity, ready for work.

"All right, let's go right into the big number," I said, swinging Meredith around by the hair. Meredith hated the big number. It was my equivalent of the bomb. "It's for your own good," I assured her.

"I really don't see how it's for my own good, Jenifer," said Meredith, in a rare insubordinate outburst.

"Ahhh . . . time will tell," I said, fanning an invisible crystal ball with my elegant fingers. Whereas Valerie was more definitive with her threats—*Do it or I'll punch your lights out*—I went for witchy and ominous. Sufficiently convinced that I could predict her future and alter it mysteriously, Meredith sailed into the blocking for "You Are Woman, I Am Man," the romantic turning point in *Funny Girl.* In my book, *Funny Girl* beat the Bible for wisdom and life lessons. I'd been to Sunday school. I'd played a hamantasch in the Purim parade, and although I genuinely admired them, I never really connected on a gut level to Ruth and Esther. Was there a Rachel? As far as I was concerned, Barbra Streisand's performance in *Funny Girl* contained every life lesson a girl needed to know. I considered it my God-appointed duty to pass on this wisdom to the Younger.

"Do I have to wear the mustache?" Meredith asked. Meredith played Nick Arnstein, Streisand's movie husband, a greasy cheat.

"You disappoint me, Nicky," I said, tapping my nails against the door frame. Meredith fetched the Nick Arnstein mustache from my vanity and sighed as I lowered the needle of my close-and-play onto the movie soundtrack. We did the whole number without stopping, mouthing the lyrics in a precise karaoke duet, kiss included. It went off without a hitch. When we were done, I released Nicky from my clutches, and Meredith flew as fast as she could down the hall. "We're all alone in the end," I called after her. For me, it was back to the vanity, my drawing board, where I rehearsed improvised lovers' confessions until bedtime.

As my sisters and I grew into early adolescence, my parents struggled to keep up appearances. They couldn't afford our English Tudor–style mansion in the first place—not its acres, its man-made ponds and nature trails, or its elevator. My parents had borrowed money from their parents for the down payment on Trilarch, then never stopped going to that bank. This put pressure on my mother, who was so overdrawn on her fantasy of us as the Jewish Kennedys—perfect house, powerful husband, and charmed children—she didn't have a penny left for reality shopping. And the reality was my father seemed to change jobs a lot. The guy may have had a decent toupee on his shoulders, but to me he didn't seem to know much about work. Entitlement had been the ethic of his upbringing. On some level I think my parents believed that my father was the anointed—that success would fall around him like a glitter storm if only he wore the right seersucker suit from Paul Stuart or if they shipped their children out to the most prestigious overnight summer camps in Maine.

My mother was the one who should have been wearing seersucker, but she continued to put it on my father. My mother was the one who should have run a stock options firm on Wall Street, but that was my father's expertise, she insisted, over coffee in the kitchen after school.

"I thought Daddy worked in advertising?" I said once.

"He's much too talented for advertising," she replied. "Dollars and cents are his expertise."

As far as I could tell, my father's only expertise was marshmallow fudge. Sometimes late at night, I found my father in the kitchen boiling Marshmallow Fluff together with Hershey bars. Then he'd pour it all in a pan and watch it harden.

"Want some fudge, little girl?" he'd ask, standing in his bathrobe.

"No, thank you, Daddy," I'd say, making off with a Twinkie or two.

Putting my father first—living for him—had left my mother with a deep need to talk. I was her go-to girl.

After school, I tried teaching her the new math: *Take one hundred percent of a mother's greatness and project it onto the father—that leaves how much for Mother?*

"Why don't you go to law school, Mommy?" I asked, echoing a dream I knew she had for herself.

"It's too late for me," she said.

"Are you happy being married to Daddy?" I said, sipping coffee, swallowing grounds.

"It's better than a poke in the eye with a sharp stick," she said. *Wuthering Heights* my parents' marriage wasn't, I'd realized. I knew my father's type, but I loved him anyway.

It all came down to pot holders in September. A few weeks after I started eighth grade, my parents, sisters, brother, and I began campaigning in earnest for my father's election to the Harrison School Board of Education. Saturday mornings we stood like the First Family in front of Vaccaro's grocery store, dressed in our navy blue turtlenecks and gray slacks, handing out pot holders stamped with VOTE FOR GENE to shoppers. The pot holders had been my father's idea—an ingenious political device, he thought.

"Every time someone reaches for a pot or a pan, they'll think of me," he explained during our ride to the shopping center. It was the kind of subliminal advertising a candidate couldn't buy, he said.

"Hello, Mrs. Kelly," I said, extending a pot holder to Mrs. Kelly and her son, my friend Timmy, who came out of Vaccaro's pushing two huge carts full of groceries.

"Well, hello, Jenifer. What have we here?" asked Mrs. Kelly.

"A pot holder," I said.

"My, my, isn't that something? Look, Tim, a pot holder."

"Oh, yeah, just what I always wanted," he said, rolling his eyes. I loved Timmy Kelly. He was the most popular boy in my grade. His mom was my friend, too. When I went to Timmy's house to play, I usually ended up in the kitchen, where Mrs. Kelly asked me to call her Shannon and we talked about marriage over coffee.

"And who are you going to vote for next week, Mrs. Kelly?" I asked her.

"Well, now, Jenifer, I haven't quite made up my mind," she said. "I sure do wish you were running for the board of education." Now, that was strange. Shannon Kelly and I were pretty close. Why was she so reluctant to show support for my father? I was about to ask her when my radar picked up a strange frequency. I turned my attention to a small, deserted area, a tiny patio set back from the main entrance to Vaccaro's. My father was there, locked in an intense, whispered conversation with a woman I'd seen before. The mole on the woman's face looked very familiar. It was the kind of mole you couldn't buy at Polk's. *Right,* I thought, she was that reporter for *The Harrison Independent,* our local newspaper weekly. *Hmmm* . . . and my father had gone to the *Independent* offices the three previous Sundays to answer her questions about his political platform. He'd been there all day.

I wondered, could her questions and his answers have possibly filled up three long Sunday afternoons when, with all due respect, I could have summed up my father's political platform in a haiku?

I think I was born with supersonic vision, kind of like those submarine radars. I couldn't help seeing beyond the parameters of normal. *Deet-deet-deet. Deet-deet-deet.* That autumn morning in front of Vaccaro's, one whole horrible panorama came into focus. I saw my mother smiling in a Chanel suit like Jackie, putting voters at ease. I saw my sisters, Alison, Valerie, and Meredith, and my brother, Noah, handing out pot holders for a man they believed in. I wondered if my father was having an affair with that lady. Valerie always told me that I saw things first, knew them first, and did them first. She wondered if I knew how lucky I was to possess such gifts. I wondered if Valerie knew that all I ever wanted was to catch a bomb.

Over the next months, Valerie's obsession with Honda minibikes reached a crescendo. After school, privileged neighborhood kids would ride their minibikes and go-carts around Trilarch in a wild, unsupervised motocross. Although I was deathly scared of Valerie's minibike, which was basically a motorcycle for children, I promised her that I would test-drive our neighbors' less intimidating go-cart. It was a shot heard round the world when on my first run I crashed the go-cart head-on into a tree, transforming Trilarch into Bilarch in an instant. Meredith was first on the scene.

"Are you okay?" she asked.

I stared straight ahead for minutes, they told me, silent and unblinking. They say I sat motionless under my white mushroom motorcycle helmet until twilight came, long after our friends had gone home. There was the undeniable impact of girl meeting tree. But the sight of a more serious accident up ahead threw me into shock. *You know things first.* I knew that my father was going to leave my mother. I didn't know what my mother was going to do about that. Neither did my grandmother Rosenberg.

The familiar whiff of L'Air du Temps mixed with peppermint Chiclets told me that Grandma Rosenberg was in the house early one Sunday morning. I followed my nose down our grand front staircase to the third step from the bottom, where I settled in for some serious eavesdropping. My grandma and my parents were hunkered down in the library, a wood-paneled room right off the entryway, where we watched TV. By the time I had adjusted my supersonic hearing—*come in, please*—they were deep in conversation. The cadence of my grandma's voice was different from usual—a clue. She was being very forceful. My mother was crying. That was always tricky—my mother had different cries for different occasions. This was her most heartbreaking, the Desdemona, clue number two.

"I need time, Eleanor," my father said. "I need my own space. Not permanently—just for now." His voice was tinny and weird. He was definitely lying to my grandmother, clue number three.

"That's crap, mister. You can't fool me," Grandma bit back. "There's only one thing that takes a man away from his family—"

"Gene is thinking of leaving, Ma. He wanted you to know first," my mother's voice wavered and cracked. Then I lost transmission. *Come in, please. Come in.* Nothing. But I had a lot of material to work with. There was the scene on the patio behind Vaccaro's . . . and now three more clues. I did as I felt I must. I made the call: It was Gene Estess in the library with a candlestick, in a reporter girlfriend, perhaps? I ran like Paul Revere up the stairs and through my sisters' rooms. "Divorce . . . divorce . . . divorce!" I yelled. I ran through Alison's room looking for Valerie.

"Maybe you could knock first," Alison said. Our oldest sister was easily annoyed by my histrionics and mad that I'd recently broken her prized Chinese wind chimes. A daughter of the counterculture, Alison spent the vast majority of her time kissing, and more, with boys; sketching in her Hippie Notebook, 1975; and filling out forms for her early admission to Brandeis University, the Angela Davis school. Alison always had one foot out the door.

"What's up?" asked Valerie, meeting me outside her room. Joni Mitchell played on her stereo.

"Divorce," I said, trying to catch my breath. "Daddy's leaving."

"Really?" Meredith met us there.

"I heard it. I knew it. I heard it. I knew it—" I was hyperventilating. It was my first anxiety attack since I was eight, when I thought my father was fooling around with the baby-sitter. I had made myself throw up that day so I could stay home from school to be near my mother.

"Get ahold of yourself," said Valerie.

"That's what you get for eavesdropping, Jenifer," said Alison, who had joined us in the hall. She was crying.

"Get in the car and wait for me," Valerie said. "Everyone, now." Alison complied, Valerie grabbed Noah, and the five of us piled into our gray Chevy Vega. Valerie ordered Alison to drive, Alison put the pedal to the metal, and we escaped from Trilarch. We had an emergency picnic. Alison made the requested pit stops according to our every desire along the way: tuna on a bed from Milk Maid, turkey on a roll with Russian and coleslaw from Butler Brothers, hot dogs from Walter's. We parked across the street from Walter's in Larchmont and headed with our food up a hill to the grassy knoll where we made family history. No one had seen the bullet hit, but we children had been blown away by the news of our parents' divorce. I loved my parents being together. It was hard to imagine my world any other way.

As Alison practiced transcendental meditation on her private patch of grass—"I have to get home for a five o'clock date," she reminded us—our baby brother, Noah, wandered off to gather rocks. That left the three of us together on the hill. As the sky darkened, Valerie,

Meredith, and I made an eternal pact there. We swore that nothing would ever break us apart. No divorce or hurricane, no national emergency or act of God. No one would break our will or our bond.

"We'll march our band out, we'll beat our drum," said Valerie. It gave me chills hearing Valerie quote from *Funny Girl*.

"And if we're fanned out?" I asked.

"You get up to the plate and try again," Valerie said. "Or I bat for you, or you bat for Meredith, or Meredith bats for me. Whoever can step up, steps up."

The old hierarchy that had Valerie beating on me and me beating on Meredith had suddenly outlived its usefulness. On the grassy knoll, it occurred to us that if we were to survive, let alone succeed, we'd need to become one another's hearts and minds, mentors—not tormentors—mutually and unconditionally. Each of us would have the other two checking in at all times, making sure, protecting, and inspiring. This dinghy wasn't going down.

"We have to go out into the world and prove we're still a family," said Meredith.

"That is correct," said Valerie, beaming.

Valerie retired her coach's whistle that day and, at age fifteen, set about the more complicated job of raising Meredith and me. After my father moved out and my mother lay down for a long rest, after Alison drove north to Brandeis University and Noah turned into a Ping-Pong ball ending up far away in my father's court, Valerie took over our care and feeding. She drove Meredith and me to school and out for dinner. She gave us money from her waitressing jobs and helped us with our homework. She did my homework when I played her right.

When my father packed up his Styrofoam toupee stand, I knew he was leaving for good. He left us without any way back to him. He grew a beard, bought a pea green Cadillac, and drove into his next life. It was like he was in the witness protection program. I was crushed when he left. He was the only man I'd known. My mother depended on him, and I loved her so much. My mother took the divorce the hardest. She spent most of her time the next year wearing Lollipop underwear and smoking in bed. She took a lot of Valium. Still, I was struck by her uncommon beauty. No one, not even Diane Keaton in *Annie Hall,* looked that good in an undershirt.

I tried coaxing her out of her room for meals, but she was seriously depressed. My mother's Kennedy dreams had exploded in her face. Her Camelot had collapsed like a house of jokers. Her magnificent clothes hung in her closet like corpses, constant reminders of her failure as a wife. She didn't deserve that rap, not for a second. The turn of events had been unfair. The burden he left her, the children he left her, the house on the brink of foreclosure—all of it was unfair and unjust. But there wasn't a court in the land that ruled on this sort of thing. Unfairness was a fact of life. Still, I wished my mother would put on some lipstick.

"Jenifer, please bring me my medicine and a glass of water," she said as I sat on the edge of her bed.

"There's pizza."

"All I want is to pull the covers over my head," she said, sliding into her ocean of a bed. She was unavailable for further comment for about two years.

By that time, my sisters and I were deep into high school. Valerie was president of the senior class. My sisters and I had taken after-school jobs at the local meat market and my favorite, Clover Donuts, a coffee shop. You should have seen me flipping those donuts, boy. I was pretty good at eating them, too. If food was a comfort to my family before the divorce, it became a savior now. My sisters and I didn't do drugs—we did the twenty-four-hour Pathmark in Yonkers, where we set land-speed records for consumption of Entenmann's chocolate chip crumb loaf at four o'clock in the morning.

By the age of fifteen, I was making decent pocket money at three Clover Donuts locations in White Plains, managing the counter and the grill. Just as Valerie had taught us, the work and resulting paycheck made me feel really accomplished. I probably could have lived without the two-a-day Bavarian cremes—where was the "a" in *creme* anyway, Valerie wanted to know. Learning to make good coffee, keeping a clean store, developing friendships with the truly handsome cops who were Clover regulars—all of this felt satisfying. I had taken my personal best from my room to the road, only now I was being paid for it. I was a working girl now, a Clover Girl. While

Cover Girl was my first choice by far—no question I had the skin for it—I was grateful for my gig.

Meredith didn't last long at the meat market. The guy who owned it was kind of a maniac. Scrub as she did, Meredith couldn't quite clean the slicing machine to his liking. She quit after two weeks. Meredith was growing up to be so beautiful—she had that Linda Carter–TV miniseries look about her that I respected so much. Valerie and I were the waitresses, the heavy lifters of the family. Meredith became our princess.

The princess and I became best friends. We ruled the breezeway, the hallway in our high school that separated the women from the girls. I taught Meredith hair. She taught me Frye boots, huge hoop earrings, and Levi's corduroys. Meredith became my absolute last word on The Look. Her fashion instincts may have even surpassed my mother's. The up-and-coming designer Calvin Klein was Meredith's idol. She followed Calvin like I followed Frank Sinatra. A great day for me was taking Meredith to Bloomingdale's and buying her a little—very little—something Calvin with my Clover money. Meredith and I had all the same friends. The front door of Trilarch, which had been closed to all but the occasional delivery from Harrison Chemists, was flung open for a never-ending party with our mutual friends, who quickly became family. Trilarch became *the* party house, as supervised by Valerie. She or I would often arrive home from work to find the action in full swing.

High school was the best time of my life. You'd think

that one of my parent's taking a powder and the other one's swallowing it in pill form would've been a setback. It did take a piece of my heart. Life with Father and Mother had been exciting. There was Angela Lansbury in *Mame,* car trips to Washington, D.C., and Boston, Bette Midler at the Palace, dinner at La Caravelle when we were the only kids in the restaurant. But when the bill came due, no one was there to pay it. Now that I was working, I wanted to make a lot of money so I could share it with my sisters. I decided I was going to buy us all a huge house in Malibu one day for our husbands, our children, and friends passing through. My boyfriend Michael told me that his uncle Harold had bought himself quite a house on the beach in Malibu.

"One day we're gonna live in Malibu, my treat," I announced to Valerie and Meredith one night, as Valerie sat at the kitchen table writing my latest English report, "The Forest as a Symbol in Shakespeare's Comedies." (She came up with the idea for the paper, too.) *I saw things first*: I was probably going to act in plays, I thought, make some movies—maybe one day my sisters and I could start our own movie studio.

As my basic training came to an end, I felt a new energy. My childhood and early education had left me with a well-earned excitement for the future. The lessons I'd learned about love, work, and what it meant to be a family gave me direction. They were lessons in granite, true lessons. I'd always had big, big dreams—now I had the means for achieving them.

"So, what do you think, Valerie—a house on the beach—"

"I'm working here, do you mind?" she said.

"Do you think I'll get us a place in Malibu?" I asked.

"I know I'm counting on it," said Meredith. She was waiting for Valerie to write her a note explaining to the homeroom teacher why Meredith had missed the previous two full days of school. Valerie had written many notes excusing Meredith and me from school. They were all lies, of course. But Valerie was really mad about this one. Without asking Valerie, Meredith had taken the family car and spent two days camping in the forests of northern Westchester with Peter Hulbert, a gorgeous West Point cadet who would capture our little sister's imagination forever.

"I bet I know what happened in *that* forest," I said. Meredith laughed. Valerie didn't laugh.

"You want a house on the beach?" Valerie said, rising from the kitchen table and coming toward me. She was so mad. "You want to live your own life and call your own shots? Do you want to make a difference in this world?" She was up in our faces.

"Yes, Valerie," Meredith and I said in unison, mockingly. We were teenagers now. We were going our separate ways, together.

"Then go deeper," she said. Valerie stormed out of the kitchen, ran up the stairs, and slammed her door closed.

Chapter Four

Y OU HAVE TO LOVE what you have in the time that you have. Okay, so it wasn't Malibu, but the Westhampton Beach rental my mother treated my sisters and me to that summer in 1997, two months after my diagnosis, wasn't chopped liver, either. It was a pretty house with a swimming pool and a short drive to the beach—and I loved it. In my heart I knew that Westhampton was the last time we would be free as a family. It was the last summer I'd pass as another lucky thirty-five-year-old loving the Hamptons.

The hammer of my ALS diagnosis had fallen in April, but I still wasn't showing overt signs of physical loss. To look at me you couldn't tell anything was wrong. Walking had become a little harder, but I still ran errands on Main Street. Getting up from low patio chairs around the pool was hard, but I still got right up from every other kind of chair. I began noticing subtle physical changes when I was alone. ALS was a real creep that way. It waited until I was alone so it could whisper in my ear. It whispered to me when I was shaving my legs.

The downstairs bathroom at Westhampton was one I would have designed for my dream house. It had a big glass-enclosed shower and marble tiles. I couldn't wait to steam things up in there. I shampooed and sang. I shaved my left leg. It was tan and elegant and so smooth. Truth be told, the muscle atrophy caused by ALS had my legs looking so very slim. Boy, did I ever love my left leg, all of a sudden. When it came time for me to swing my right leg up onto the marble shelf, I couldn't—quite—do it. I tried kicking it up again, but no go. Okay, so . . . I wouldn't shave my right leg. European women didn't shave either leg and everyone still loved them. This was where having a degenerative disease got a little tricky. ALS would take away something relatively small—shaving my right leg— knowing that I would immediately rationalize the loss. Nature designed human beings to rationalize loss. We are programmed to make comforting excuses for ourselves when painful things happen. Without rationalization, we'd all go off the deep end.

I rationalized my experience in the shower. Although I couldn't shave my right leg, I figured I still looked healthier than ever. My hair, my tan . . . I didn't *look* sick. People said I'd never looked better. I probably had a slow-moving form of ALS. There was such a thing, I'd been told. Even if there wasn't, I knew that if anyone could set a new precedent for the disease, I could. The brochures from Dr. Rowland's nurse didn't begin to describe the woman in *my* mirror. They had photographs of people tilted back in wheelchairs with tubes and machines coming out of them. They had oatmeal recipes for patients who couldn't swallow solid food, and line illustrations of clawed hands. The printed materials were so "complete dependence." They didn't describe me for a second, and they looked like they were printed in 1950. After a glorious summer in the sun, my sisters and I would find other brochures, consider new medical perspectives, and gather second and third opinions.

In the meantime, I was loving every moment. *No one, nothing, will break us.* I swam with the kids in the pool all summer. I held them in the water. I ate Meredith's guacamole, the best on earth, and I put on lipstick. I drank hot coffee by the pool in the morning and danced with the kids at night. I didn't have children of my own, but my sisters gave me theirs. The children and I were so in love with each other. The guys, Jake and Willis, were a midget Butch Cassidy and the Sundance Kid, with Jake, Meredith's oldest, the sultry five-year-old leader, and Willis, the sunshine. There was a girl on the scene now, Jane, who would be Meredith's middle child. Jane was two. I watched Jane play on a brilliant orange beach towel. Her eyes were the color of purple Tootsie Pops, just like her mother's. The colors that summer: Jane's eyes, the red of tomatoes, the blue sky and the pool, the greens and chocolate browns of lettuces that had just been pulled from the ground. Colors stood out as never before. This was what I stood to lose, the amazing colors of life.

My friends were all over the Hamptons that summer. Martha, Geoffrey, and Merrill came by for a visit in their red rented convertible, top down. Martha brought the world's freshest salmon to cook that night. The guys wanted iced coffees. Jane watched Martha prepare foil packets of salmon and summer vegetables while Geoff, Merrill, and I drove in to town. I wanted to pick up something for the kids. I loved getting them a little something from town.

"Are you crazy, Jenifer?" said Meredith, when she'd see the daily shopping bags from town filled with candy and toys for them.

"It's just a little something," I'd say. "Relax."

Driving with Geoff and Merrill on a sunny, breezy afternoon in Westhampton made me feel powerful, as if a miracle could happen at any minute. My guys looked buff in the front seat, with their tank tops and their tans. I was the babe in the back. My dark hair blew proud like a flag in the breeze. We had our sunglasses on. Someone should have taken a picture.

It was funny. I was definitely different from my friends—I was building an individual life for myself. I was creating my own way. But being with Martha, Geoff, and Merrill reminded me how much I loved being part of the crowd. Pursuing individuality was important. It was crucial to my happiness. But I felt proud blending in, too. I loved being a part of things, playing in all the reindeer games. I loved participating. As Geoff and Merrill hopped out of the car for coffee, I struggled to get out of the backseat. My legs were like posts. A wave of exhaustion washed over me. I thought that I was going to faint, so I waved the guys on and stayed in the car. I saw the candy store and the toy store a few feet away from me. They were so close yet so far away. I wanted to hop out of the car and shop, but I couldn't.

"Come on, Jen," said Geoff. He felt scared to see me still sitting there when he came back to the car with his coffee.

"I feel a little weird," I said.

"Walking might be good for you," he said, offering me his arms. I didn't think so. I had started wearing plastic braces for walking. They were supposed to prevent my feet from dragging on the ground. The braces didn't work very well. All they seemed to do was make my calves sweat profusely. I felt the plastic rubbing against them in the heat.

"Tomorrow's another day," said Martha, rationalizing my trip to town over salmon and chardonnay. I loved my friends. They loved me so much. I worried about tomorrow. I went shopping with Valerie and Meredith at our favorite fruit and vegetable stand. The uneven ground presented new obstacles to my walking and balancing. But Martha had been right. Tomorrow was another day. I was able to get out of our car. I relied on my inner Valerie, Jenifer, and Meredith to get me through. *Steady,* I thought, approaching the stand decked out in luscious fruits. *Just get to the avocados. Walk over to the avocados slowly and pick one up. Good girl. Excellent.* I brought my bag of avocados over to Meredith, who had chosen sensational peaches and nectarines. Valerie paid. The whole thing went off without a hitch. We bought. I blended in. As far as the world was concerned, I was just another woman shopping for her family. I loved that.

For two straight months, Scott manned the barbecue. It was hard for me to picture him anywhere except hovering over sea bass or thick steaks grilling. He cooked every single thing perfectly to order. There were fights that summer, and wine, and a lot of laughing. We watched fireworks from the patio as the Fourth of July came and went. Jake swam in the deep end for the first time. One night, after Meredith had run from the dinner table nauseated, she announced that she was pregnant. Then in August the waves started coming regularly. The weird wave of exhaustion that I'd experienced in town that afternoon with my friends came back. The waves drove me to my bed, where they broke and washed over me. My bed was no longer a place for sleeping or watching TV or making love. It was my hiding place.

Rationalizing became all the rage that summer. Everyone was doing it. Valerie and Meredith were determined to spin gold from Dr. Rowland's diagnosis. They were sure I had a remarkably slow-moving case, and they heartily endorsed the program of physical therapy that had been prescribed by the same nurse who'd given me the brochures. Physical therapy didn't make much sense to me. The nerve cells in my spine and brain were dying. My muscles were drying up. I didn't need to work out. I needed medicine, fast.

"Georgia says you're the strongest ALS patient she's ever seen," said Meredith as I lay on my bed, completing a series of leg lifts prescribed by a jaunty physical therapist who was well-meaning but knew nothing of ALS. I had always wanted to have a daughter and name her Georgia. Instead, I got a physical therapist named Georgia. My muscles shook and fasciculated as I lifted the light weights strapped to my ankles. The kids watched, fascinated.

"Go, Jen Jen," Jake cheered. I dripped sweat.

"This is totally stupid," I said, lifting my ton of bricks. "You can't get better from what I have." I couldn't blame my sisters for believing that a course of exercise might buy me a little time. No evidence to the contrary existed. But I was starting to feel frustrated. The general perception out there, especially among people who love you, is that if you try very hard, you can make yourself better. But there are things in life and death that are beyond our control. The power of positive thinking extends only so far. Walking on burning coals, for example—I could see where that was totally doable, at least during the first year of ALS. Overcoming a fatal, totally untreatable illness through exercise and eating right seemed like a bit of a stretch.

"Peter says you've never looked healthier or more beautiful. You *know* he doesn't lie," said Meredith. My little sister and her West Point cadet had married. Meredith and Peter were our family's version of Elizabeth Taylor and Richard Burton, our resident jungle cats. They fought and made up like nobody's business. Peter was air for Meredith to breathe. I've felt that way about a couple of guys in my life, but Meredith was married to it, body and soul. Peter was my brother. We had known each other for a long time.

"Let's go to the beach, Jenny," he said one afternoon as I held my iced tea glass poolside. I had navigated much of civilized Westhampton successfully, but I was scared of the beach, mostly because of the sand. And the bathing suits. "Nonsense, Jenny. Let's go see the sunset."

I leaned on Peter as we walked from the parking lot to the edge of the beach. "Look at the sun," Peter said, turning his face to catch the last few rays. We settled onto the sand.

"You realize it's gonna take a miracle to get through this," I said.

"What would life be without miracles, Jenny?" Peter said, and the sun was gone. I couldn't get up. Peter lifted me partway, then I pitched forward onto my knees. Sky, sand, and water merged, then separated into distinct bands of color. I knelt before the totem of colors and prayed for a miracle. It was getting cold.

"Let's go home, Jenny," said Peter. He picked me up and carried me in his arms to firm ground. We had to get home for dinner. Meredith was making sea bass. Scott was grilling.

Princess Diana died that summer. I remember watching television late one night when the news broke. I was the first one in the house to hear about the tragedy, and I was Paul Revere again, waking people up, telling them about a woman who was my age, whom my sisters and I had admired, who had died in a terrible car accident. I loved Diana's face. I felt a strange twinge of relief at the news of her death. The tragedy comforted me, in the same way my friend John Kennedy's death did later on, and not in a misery-loves-company kind of way. I felt that if Diana and John were brave enough to go to the other side, I was, too. I gained strength thinking about them. If I was going to be blending in with a new crowd one day, I could do worse than those two. I imagined what it would be like meeting them on the other side.

The summer was over in a second. The last night, from my bedroom just off the patio, I could hear my family all around me. Jake and Willis were laughing. My sisters and their husbands talked logistics for the trip home. Although I longed to be a part of the conversation, I was drawn to rest. For the first time, I felt a distance between my family and me. The disease was whispering to me again. The next morning, I put on my lug-soled Gucci loafers, the only footwear I felt safe wearing, and walked down the front steps for the drive home to Manhattan. I went down with a bang. It was a bad fall. Meredith came running and screaming.

"Oh my God, you tripped on the avocado," she said.

"What?" I said, dazed and totally confused.

"You tripped . . . the avocado," she said, indicating a dried-up avocado peel in a gutter on the other side of the driveway.

"You don't trip on an avocado, you slip, and I didn't slip, I fell because I can't walk," I said.

None of us was ready for the fall. When my family dropped me off at my apartment after the summer, I could have been any other single woman coming home from her Hamptons share. As I stepped out of Meredith and Peter's car, I noticed the colors change: Summer red turned into sidewalk gray; sky blue turned into taxi yellow, and Tootsie-Pop purple, the color of Jane's eyes, became the drab fluorescent white of my vestibule. This was the light that would guide me from the car and my family's unforgettable summer into the autumn. Valerie and Meredith stayed in the car as I walked in to my building. We were starting to realize that there were journeys I'd have to take alone. I pulled myself up by the banister, step-by-step, to my apartment. I didn't look back. *No hurricane, no act of God will break us.* I was already focused on the job ahead. In my heart I knew that in order to fight ALS, I'd have to come up with a force at least as strong. That force was my love with my sisters, my best thing.

"I still think we can get out of this," Meredith had said

as I'd struggled through Georgia's grueling physical ther-apy regimen that summer. And that became my sisters' and my mantra: *I still think we can get out of this.* As my body changed, my sisters and I would say it over and over. But the truth was that even if my sisters and I didn't get out of ALS, we'd get out of it. Does that make any sense? It made sense to me my first night back on Seventy-first Street, as I walked carefully to my bed and lay there in the dark fantasizing and fasciculating for hours. This was what I wanted to say to my sisters and what I hoped they would always remember: Even if I died soon, our love would roam the earth like a kind, three-headed monster. I wanted to tell them that we would prevail, as family, as one, eternally. It may sound queer, but I knew I was born to love. Love had gotten me through my first summer of ALS, and I was betting my heart it would take me further. All I had to do was go deeper.

Chapter Five

I WAS NEVER that great a student, academically speaking. When September rolled around, my best thing was buying new notebooks with my sisters at Big Top and sticking Wacky Packages on them. I remember being very hardworking the first days of third grade. I arranged my pencils and sharpener in a new carrying case and carefully laid out my next day's outfits on top of my bureau. I listened hard in class and wrote down everything my teachers said. I was adamant about completing my homework with precision and neatness.

"Wanna play Barbies?" asked Meredith, a mere second-grader. She stood at my door with our black patent-leather Barbie carrying cases and her mop of black hair.

"Sorry, Pigpen, I have more important things to do," I said, closing the door in her face.

My passion for academics generally lasted about two weeks. I think I started each grade *pretending* to go to school, like I was starring in a movie *about* school. Then,

when reality set in, and I recognized that third grade—
a.k.a. pure drudgery—was my fate, I totally tuned out.

"So where's my Barbie case?" I asked Meredith, who
had been staring blankly at the TV for two weeks, and
we ran upstairs for an afternoon of international fashion.
I'd like to see my social studies notebook from third
grade now, with its first two pages of meticulous notes
and the rest totally blank.

By the age of thirty-five, I had accepted that drudgery
was a part of every life. But staying in the game and taking
notes—no matter what—definitely had its payoffs. I
wasn't crazy about my current job in public relations, but
it was helping me pave my way to my next project—the
production company I was starting with Valerie and
Meredith. Autumn had become a time of year to reassess
my goals. The cool snap in the air was a starting gun:
Make the meeting; buy the shoes; call him. But when the
starting gun went off that September after my diagnosis, I
couldn't get out of a taxi by myself anymore. I couldn't run
out for a client meeting or a tuna sandwich. I couldn't run.
Elevator rides to my twentieth-floor office had become
surreal. Half of me went up while the other half stayed in
the lobby. The leg braces I'd started wearing at the end of
the summer remained more of a nuisance than a help. I
started calling in sick a lot. Then I quit my job. My best
friend, Simon Halls, came from Los Angeles to console
me the day I told my boss I was gravely ill and I'd be packing my office to leave immediately.

"You're out of there, Kitty," said Simon, raising a glass

of champagne over roasted chicken and mashed potatoes, our favorite, at Cafe Luxembourg. Simon called me "Kitty." He'd borrowed the nickname from Peter and Meredith, who had started calling each other "Kitty" when they fell in love in high school. Simon and I might as well have been married—our chemistry was that complex. I'd met Simon when he lived in New York. He'd hired me for my first job after Naked Angels, an off-Broadway theater company I'd helped run. Before Simon, I had worked for next to no money. Simon introduced me to the notion that I could make a career *and* money for myself in entertainment. He'd encouraged me to take the public relations job I'd just quit.

"It wasn't the perfect job, Kitty, but it was a total step up," he said. As Simon spoke, I took in his chocolate brown eyes and boyish hair. Even when he was rumpled, Simon was elegant. "An elegant human being," my mother had dubbed him. I found him intoxicating at times. Simon was the champagne of men, and he was brutally honest with me. We hadn't seen each other since my diagnosis. I was afraid that he was going to notice a big change in my walking and say so.

"Look at you, Kitty. You're doing so well," Simon said as we made our way back to my apartment, arm in arm, after dinner. He pulled me close to him.

"I can't walk, Kitty," I said. I called Simon "Kitty," too.

"What do you call *this,* Kitty?" he said.

"Walking," I said, "v-e-r-y slowly."

"Slow is good, Kitty," he said, laughing. "Silly Kitty."

Simon and the night air smelled so good. After he dropped me off, I collapsed on my couch. But the night was young. Buoyed by champagne and Simon's encouraging words, I decided to run a few neurological tests of my own. I'd been playing games with myself most nights to see how fast my ALS was moving. I stood on my tiptoes reaching toward the high cabinet over my refrigerator. I touched it. I filled a coffee mug with water and carried it back and forth across my living room floor without spilling it. I sat down at my table and got up and sat down and got up. If a chair wasn't too low to the ground—my dining room chair wasn't—I was still okay getting to my feet. Maybe I had what Dr. Rowland said we were hoping for, a quirky case. I prayed nightly for the quirkiest, slowest-moving ALS case in history. Unfortunately, I failed the tweezers test. For the first time, I couldn't grip them. *Good-bye, tweezers.* ALS forced me to say good-bye to at least one thing every week. This week it was my job and tweezers.

The next morning I headed out with my new cane to deposit my last paycheck. Canes work fashion-wise, if you're Simon Halls or Fred Astaire. With its shiny black metal shaft and rubber-tipped bottom, mine had an undeniably orthopedic look about it, but if I wanted to avoid a repeat of the phantom avocado incident in Westhampton, I had to use it. Navigating my neighborhood had become quite an adventure. I suddenly had trouble opening the front door to the Muffin Shop, where I'd developed a satisfying flirtation not only with the muffins but with a guy named Phil from my block. That morning, Phil's rosy face screwed up with concern as I struggled with the door. He didn't know what to make of the cane.

"Hey, Jenny, how ya doin'?" Phil asked, making room for me at his table. I will never forget the warmth of the Muffin Shop, the mixture of steam from the coffee and hot muffins that always pulled me in from the cold. The Muffin Shop was our kind of sauna, Phil and me.

"Flu's got me," I said. "Some kind of weird flu." I grabbed my bag to go and headed for the exit. "Bank time," I said.

"You gonna rob one?"

"You and me, Phil," I said.

"Take care, Jenny," said Phil, winking. I never saw him again.

Something bad was happening. My inalienable rights to life, liberty, and the pursuit of errands in my own neighborhood were being violated by ALS. I crossed Columbus Avenue to the dry cleaners, where I picked up my favorite black suit, a sleek, stunning creature. I was so happy to see it. Gripping my cane and bag in my right hand, I slung it over my left shoulder. "All right, let's do it," I ordered my body, which ignored me. Like me at a school dance, my body seemed unable to initiate anything. I stood motionless on the sidewalk for minutes, not knowing how to make the first move toward Citibank, my last stop before going home. *Put one foot in front of the other.* By the time I got to the bank entrance, my Guccis felt like cement blocks. Because the muscles around my feet had weakened, I was having trouble lifting them for my next steps. It took me a good hour to snake my way through the bank line, but the teller finally handed me my pink deposit slip. It was like getting a medal at the Olympics.

Since when do muffins weigh a hundred pounds? As I turned onto my block, my dry cleaning weighed down on me. I hoisted the hanger into the crook of my neck as I fought on, but I wasn't going to make it after all. My street was deserted and Phil was nowhere in sight, so I unburdened myself. As I continued unsteadily toward my apartment, I let go of my muffin bag, I let go of my suit in its plastic wrap, I let go of my deposit slip. Piece by piece, my morning fell to the sidewalk like leaves. By the time I got inside, it was dark all around. I fell on my bed. New York was my city. My sisters and I worked there. My friends and I had closed it down a few times. New York was where I had made some big mistakes and where I was making my mark as a producer, a mover, a shaker, and as a woman who was ready to move with her family to a quiet apartment overlooking the most incredible city in the world. I dialed Valerie.

"I can't live alone anymore," I said. "My city . . ."

"That's okay," Valerie said. "Everything's going to be okay." We stayed on the phone a long time, just listening.

Valerie and I packed the things I'd be needing into boxes, and I moved back to Harrison, the town of my youth. I had always fantasized about returning to Harrison one day. It was a high school reunion fantasy with my fellow graduates collectively gasping as I whisked in to the hotel ballroom at the top of my game. I'd be more beautiful than they had remembered, and verging on fame. Between bites of bad beef Stroganoff, I'd entertain them with photos of my children and stories from the set of my latest production, a comedy about sisters. Then I'd whisk out, more beautiful to my classmates than when I had whisked in.

My actual return to Harrison wasn't as auspicious by half. Meredith, Peter, Jake, and Jane lived in Harrison in a modern ranch-style home. It seemed so perfect that Meredith and Peter had moved back to Harrison when they married. It was the place where they had first laid eyes on each other. Meredith and Peter had returned to Harrison to build something of their own. And now I was moving in. My biggest fear was burdening Meredith and her family and basically ruining their lives. ALS was a family disease. It wanted to cut everyone down. But you don't cut Meredith down so easily.

Meredith was my little sister, but in many ways she grew up being the toughest of us. Unlike Valerie and me, Meredith didn't talk up, down, and around a subject. Valerie and I had the gift of gab—Meredith had the gift of go. She landed the plane. Plus Meredith was just plain great to look at. No one knew how she did it—maybe she shopped when everyone was sleeping—but Meredith always managed to walk in with that one great new shirt or those pants or boots that made you notice. There she was in the driveway to meet me the day I moved in. She looked like the Statue of Liberty, with her upright, broad-shouldered frame and eyes that could cut diamonds. From the car I could smell dinner cooking.

I would hit my emotional bottom during my stay at Meredith's house, probably because it was the safest place on earth for me to do it. If Martha Stewart ever does a roundup of the most fashionable rooms for facing down one's mortality, she'll want to feature my room in Meredith and Peter Hulbert's house in Harrison. The Hulberts converted their storage room into a private bedroom and bathroom with pretty pastel soaps just for me. Meredith put in carpeting and a firm new bed, and dressed it in Ralph Lauren and puffy pillows. She had made sure that if I was going to be spending more time in bed, mine was fit for a queen.

My sisters and I had always taken care of one another, but I was about to rely on Meredith big time. I felt inhibited being so needy. As the older sister, I felt much more comfortable taking care of her, giving her advice when she and Peter fought, and devising business strategies together. Now I was going to be waited on by my younger sister, who had two young kids with another on the way. My body started tanking as soon as I got there. It was as if it had been waiting for me to get to a safer place before it fell apart. Meredith cooked healthful meals for me. She cleaned my room every ten minutes, she held my arm as we walked up and down her street together, and she kept me in fresh flowers.

"I feel like I'm living in a hotel," I said to her. She provided me with every conceivable comfort and convenience around the clock.

"Some hotel," she said, rolling her eyes. Meredith worked hard at being a wife and mother, and she had the kids to show for it. Jake and Jane were fine children, just great human beings. They would be my saviors over the next ten months. The way they looked and smelled and walked and talked—they satisfied my senses. They made me feel alive with love. I worked to stay strong so that I could make them proud.

"Jane, get off the bed!" Meredith screamed, running in with a knife from the kitchen. She'd been chopping vegetables for a stir-fry.

"No, Mer, I love it," I said. The kids were my air. They were like puppies jumping on my bed and nuzzling me. I held them and they held me back.

"Stay here forever, Jen Jen," said Jake.

"Stay here forever, Den Den," said Jane. When Scott, Valerie, and Willis came up to Harrison, I'd have the three kids in my room. Jake, Willis, Jane, and I would go shopping on the computer. I bought them toys. I bought them a lot of toys. Those afternoons were educational, too. I taught the children how to order anything they wanted online using my credit card.

"Are you crazy, Jenifer?" asked Valerie, surveying the latest shipment of cartons from Toys "R" Us.

"It's just a little something," I said.

"Do you think there are worms when you die?" I asked as Meredith and I sat cross-legged on my bed eating turkey sandwiches with Russian dressing for lunch one day. "Like, do you think they crawl into your eye sockets?"

"I try not to think about worms," she said, rising from the bed with that look in her eyes. "Gotta go."

At roughly the same time that I started becoming obsessed with worms and skeletons, Meredith developed wicked morning sickness. She could be seized at any moment by a volcanic nausea. We'd be deep into a conversation when Meredith, suddenly overcome, would bolt.

"See ya," I said. I felt guilty: I was sick because something was dying inside me. Meredith felt guilty: She was sick because life was growing inside her. Oy, the guilt of the sisters . . .

Despite my efforts at staying positive, my days took on a troubling shapelessness. Before I got sick, it was the momentum of my routine—working out, eating healthfully, working my butt off, and dating—that propelled me forward and gave my life meaning. Without that structure, I slid into depression. I sat on my bed, looking out the window at a big tree in Meredith's backyard. The tree had lost its leaves. Its brittle branches moved in the wind. At night the tree turned into a swaying skeleton inching toward me, arms outstretched. Thoughts of death wrapped themselves in my Ralph Lauren sheets. My pillow became a tombstone. I would fall asleep to the sound of me disappearing, all except the bones. Worms crawled through my eye sockets—

"Jen Jen," said Jake. When I woke up, Jake was sitting on my bed in his red devil costume for Halloween. If this was the devil, I suddenly wasn't scared of dying.

"I love your costume, sweet baby," I said. He smiled. Jake was the oldest of my nieces and nephews. If Simon and I had ever had a son, he would have looked like Jake.

"Are you coming trick-or-treating tonight?" he asked.

"Maybe," I said.

"Please . . ." I was tempted by the devil, but we decided I'd be better off staying in and handing out candy to visitors. Speaking of Halloween thrills and chills, my walking had gotten so bad that I'd started using an aluminum walker to get around. I had never seen a young person using one of those things. I stared at my walker parked in the corner of my room. The cold afternoon sun reflected off its aluminum sides. It was the scariest Halloween I could remember.

"Bubble gum," said Jane, waddling in. "Bubble gum."

"You want bubble gum?" I asked.

"Bubble gum," said Jane.

"Where's Mommy?"

"Bubble gum kitchen bubble gum kitchen bubble gum kitchen—"

"I get it, honey. I'll get it." Meredith had run out to the store for candy for me and the trick-or-treaters, and my baby girl wanted her gum. Balancing with my walker, and with Jane and a curious Jake in tow, I ventured out to the kitchen. The sound of that walker was really something: click-click-click, click-click-click. It was an old metal horse—a three-legged thing—probably headed for the glue factory. I made it to the kitchen counter, where I released the walker and grabbed marble. Suddenly I was Clint Eastwood hanging on to one ledge while trying to get to the next building. From there I reached up to a cabinet holding Jane's shocking pink gum dispenser and some glasses. One wrong move from me and those glasses were coming down.

"What is this stuff?" I said, handing the gum to Jane.

"Bubble gum!" said Jane, triumphant. I felt triumphant, too. Giving the children what they wanted meant everything to me.

"Say thank you," said Jake.

"Thank you, Den Den," Jane said, unraveling yard after yard of strawberry gum. We three spent the rest of the morning chewing bubble gum on my bed.

Whenever I was alone—when Peter wasn't bringing me coffee and a muffin from town, or Meredith and I weren't talking about Valerie, or Valerie and I weren't talking about Meredith, or the kids weren't playing football on my bed—the creeping thoughts returned. I thought a lot about never having children. I thought about never running my own company. The notion of *never*, which I had often fought against, made its way into my mind. The waves of exhaustion from the summer had returned and were more frequent now. I hibernated. I started sleeping later into the mornings. The sounds of the Hulberts would awake me momentarily: Peter's polished shoes against the kitchen floor before work, the garage door going up, Jake and Meredith fighting about his backpack, Andrea, the nanny, getting Jane down the front steps—clunk, clunk—in her stroller for nursery school. The sounds of my family heading out into the world were like an extra blanket that sent me back and deeper into sleep.

My friends tried to break the door down. They had been so easygoing in Westhampton only a few months before. But now they seemed impatient. I listened to their pet theories of why I had gotten sick in the first place and what I needed to do to make myself well again. My friends became guerrillas on a mission. They came up to Harrison from the city in shifts and tried to scare me into action.

"Life is a river, Kitty," my friend Merrill said, illustrating in the air. He called me "Kitty," too. "Picture this big rock in the middle of the river. The rock changes the course of the river. *You* are that rock, Kitty. *You* change the course of your illness."

"I think you've been watching too much public television, Kitty." I called Merrill "Kitty," too. He was starting to sound like that guy with the beard on Channel 13 who talked about the miracles of broccoli. Merrill and I had produced many a play together in our heyday at Naked Angels. We'd made names for ourselves turning young plays into hot, sold-out happenings. He and I had willed the masses to our theater on Seventeenth Street. As far as Merrill was concerned, we were going to will away my ALS. Other friends tried coaxing me out to dinners and parties in the city. They felt my returning to New York was the best medicine, but I couldn't bear going back. New York was the crime scene now, the place where my dreams had been shot down.

Everyone who came to visit me in Harrison brought me a book either about broccoli and being, rivers and rocks, or death and dying. One book was about stages of dying—Chapter One: Anger; Chapter Two: Denial; Chapter Three: Acceptance—as if there was a particular, predictable order to the whole process. There wasn't a word in that book about worms, nothing about the inability to reach out and hold a guy or never seeing your nephew graduate from high school. When people came to my bed with books, I asked them to please place them on the stacks on my floor. I had collected about a hundred books in short stacks. They made a great doorstop.

I started reading the obituaries instead, scouring them for mentions of other young people. Everyone in the death section was older than me: A physicist died from heart failure at ninety-three; a shipping magnate lost his battle with cancer at eighty-seven; a woman who had discovered a hidden meaning in birdsongs stroked out at seventy-six. One day I read about a young woman who had died in her early thirties from a rare form of lymphoma. She was quoted as saying that being sick was like drifting farther and farther away on a raft. She said she felt that she lived in another country. Her I could relate to.

Valerie wanted to make me better in one fell swoop. When she wasn't in Harrison helping Meredith, or psyching me up for the medicine we were somehow going to find, she was on her computer, on the Internet, learning about the latest in ALS research.

"The problem here is that the experts know nothing," she said, after she had spent three days straight visiting useless neuroscience websites. She stayed in the game, though. She kept taking notes and researching the research. Then she discovered her one fell swoop. His name was Jeffrey Rothstein, and he was an accomplished ALS researcher and clinician at Johns Hopkins University in Baltimore. Valerie had made an appointment for us to see Dr. Rothstein.

"This guy's the maverick," Valerie said. I'd already seen the giant in the field. I had nothing to lose in meeting the maverick. Valerie rationalized that there was no definitive, beyond-a-reasonable-doubt diagnosis for ALS. Maybe Rothstein's second opinion would differ from Dr. Rowland's first one. Plus, Rothstein had medicine—apparently, plenty of it—cooking in his lab. Something called *growth factors* that Valerie felt might help me.

My sisters and mother and I went to Johns Hopkins on the Amtrak. While Meredith and I ate pretzels from the bar car, Valerie laid out our dream scenario: Rothstein would examine me and tell me I didn't have ALS, or, worst case, he'd tell me I had ALS and that he was going to give me something to slow it down or stop it. Then we'd celebrate in the restaurant of the luxurious Harbor Court Hotel, where Valerie had made reservations.

"My treat," said Valerie.

"My treat," said my mother. "And pass me a pretzel." The hotel part worked out. We got a lot of great room service at the Harbor Court before my appointment at Hopkins the next morning.

In bed that night, I felt hopeful. I was a very hopeful person. I thought about high school, when my friend Timmy and I had gotten a really good laugh from that word: *hope*. It was one of those words that was so corny to say out loud: "I *hope* you're coming to my house after school, Tim." So Timmy and I made up a little play on it. When we didn't think there was a hope in hell of something happening, we'd say *hopes* or *many hopes*. If Timmy asked me if I was going to pass the geometry Regents, I'd say, "Hopes." If I asked Timmy if he was ever going to marry Nancy (my best friend who was in love with him), he'd say, "Hopes." Then my sisters started doing it. The cult of hopes followed me into adulthood:

Me: You remind me of Cary Grant, Kitty. Simon: Hopes.

Simon: You're so much prettier than Catherine Zeta-Jones, Kitty. Me: Many hopes.

I was all sarcasm when it came to hopes, but in my heart I was high on a hill, hoping that Dr. Rothstein would set me free.

"I like what he's wearing," Meredith said, as Rothstein whizzed past us in the waiting room at Hopkins. Dr. Rothstein was my age and well put together, but there was something about him that gave me a queasy feeling the instant I met him. Where Dr. Rowland had been gentlemanly, Dr. Rothstein seemed aggressive, like he couldn't wait to share the hard, cold truth with me. My whole family jammed into the tiny exam room, waiting for Jeff Rothstein to commute my sentence. He rolled over facts and figures of ALS like a lawn mower, using the paper on my exam table to illustrate the deadly pathways of the disease. His exam was different from Dr. Rowland's but just as bizarre. Dr. Rothstein used circus equipment, too—pulleys.

"No question you have ALS," said Rothstein as I closed my gown around me. He confirmed Dr. Rowland's diagnosis immediately. He was unequivocal. "Your motor neurons are dying," he said, "and they'll never be replaced."

"I don't understand," I said. "We can replace damaged hearts and kidneys. Why not motor neurons?"

"Cell transplants? That's science fiction." He smashed our questions like bugs.

"But you're developing therapies to block glutamate, right?" asked Valerie, who was starting to use words and terms that none of us had heard before. "You and your colleagues are doing important work with growth factors."

"Oh, that's all early stages," he said. Dr. Rothstein said that a cure for ALS was twenty years down the road. "People come in with questions," he said. "Unfortunately, we just don't have answers." We were stunned. I asked my family to leave the room. I had to know the effects ALS was going to have on my love life.

"Emotionally, the love might deepen," he said. "Physically, everything will change."

"What should I do?"

"Travel maybe. I had one patient who went to Paris. Some people max out their credit cards." No matter what the future held, Dr. Rothstein and I would always have Paris.

"I want you to go on with your lives," I said to my family back at our messy suite in the Harbor Court Hotel. It was way dark outside and way past checkout time. "Nothing will be the same now, but you must promise me you'll go on with your lives. If you don't live now, I'll feel worse. Everything will be worse." There wasn't much to say. The only sound was tears falling on the carpet. It had been raining in Baltimore, a cold, driving rain, from the moment we'd gotten off the Amtrak from New York the day before. I would always remember Baltimore in the rain and the sight of my sisters' defeated faces after we got our second opinion. It was a long train trip home. My sisters and I got drunk on M&M's.

I was back at Meredith's hibernating again when a tornado blew in from the East. It settled over the house and stayed for a while. It was rare winds—something I'd call a tornado of the absurd. My sisters and I got caught up in it but good. After our visit with Dr. Rothstein, with no Western solutions or any true medicine in sight, Valerie, Meredith, and I got caught up in healing options from the East. Two afternoons a week, we three devoutly Western girls drove to Long Island for my meetings with Caran (emphasis on the second syllable, naturally), a self-described psychic minister. Seriously, the woman had business cards. Caran had a healing hut, which was really just a warped toolshed behind her clapboard house. Walking to the healing hut, I could see my minister's family's underwear drying on the line.

"I hate talking about money," Caran said when she met me.

"Yeah, it's a drag," I said, leaning on my walker.

"But if you want me to rearrange your cells, it's gonna cost you," she said. Basically, Caran was a masseuse. She wasn't a bad person. The woman had kids to support.

"It's something to do," I admitted as Valerie, Meredith, and I flew down the Long Island Expressway for my twice-weekly Caran treatments. Meredith said she noticed that I might be getting a little stronger from my sessions with Caran. Valerie agreed.

"At seventy-five bucks a pop, you'd like to think so," I said.

"Hey, Caran, ya gotta lose the stoop," I said after a couple months of seeing her. I couldn't get up the cement stoop to the healing hut anymore, even with my walker.

"Stand in your legs," said Caran. "You can do it."

"I'm gonna fall on this stoop, Caran. I'm gonna fall on my ass." When we first met, Caran promised she would cure me. She sure changed her tune as I got worse.

"Only *time* will tell if you'll heal," said Caran.

"I thought *you* were gonna heal me."

"Time is wiser than I," she said. "And speaking of time, Jenifer, when might you honor your outstanding balance for November?"

Tornado-force winds knocked us back and forth. Meredith blew into my room with an open jar of truly foul-smelling paste. There had to be a dead moose in that jar.

"Are you trying to kill me?" I said as she waved it under my nose.

"Give it a chance," she said. The paste was called Amrit Kalash. It was an ancient blend of herbs from India that balanced the body and the mind. Forget what it did to your digestion.

"Get out of here with that crap," I said. Meredith cracked up. She'd been mixing it into my daily smoothies for weeks.

There was a homemade battery advertised on the Internet for stimulating my muscles. We bought that. There was the purported medicinal power of burning sage. We burned bundles. Valerie came home with bags of vitamins. I took them. One woman, who had apparently saved serious heart patients with a laying on of hands, laid her hands on me. She looked like a lemur. She jumped around on all fours on a couch. She scared me. My sisters and I were desperate. We drove everywhere, sent away for everything, anything that would make me better. We were dizzy and desperate. We were broke. There was snake oil and swamis and healers galore, and everyone took MasterCard.

I needed a diet Coke. As I walked to the kitchen on my walker, I fell backward and cracked my skull against the hardwood floor. Meredith ran in and cradled my head in her hands. "You're fine," she said. "I promise you." She lifted me into my room and onto my bed. I'm surprised she didn't give birth right there.

"I think I gotta get a wheelchair, Merry," I said, my head spinning from a slight concussion.

I called Dr. Rowland's nurse, the one who had given me the brochures. I tried relating to her woman-to-woman. She wasn't part of the tornado. She was more the Wicked Witch flying through it.

"Maybe I'm not using the right shoes," I said when we met in her office. "Maybe there's something with a negative heel—something in an Earth Shoe—that would be safer." The nurse was eating a tuna sandwich with her mouth open. *Good-bye, tuna.*

"I'm gonna say the dirty word, Miss Estess," she said. "*Wheelchair* . . . I don't want you ending up in the emergency room with broken bones." She seemed about as genuine in her concern as Nurse Ratched. "If you want

Medicaid to pay for a chair, ya gotta order now," she said. She fanned out more brochures for me on her desk. They featured huge gleaming wheelchairs with knobs and trays and scaffolding. She recommended a custom-made chair, one that could accommodate the progressive weakness, eventual paralysis, and a respirator.

"But I don't need that now," I said.

"You will," she said. "You will."

"I want to die," I said, riding shotgun as Meredith drove home.

"Not yet," Valerie said from the backseat.

"I'm ruining your lives. I'm infecting . . . everything," I said. "It's in my body . . . everywhere. I want to stop while I can still remember what everything looked like. I want to remember colors the way they were."

"So remember colors the way they were," said Meredith.

"What if I can't?"

"You wanna die?" Meredith asked.

"Yes," I said, and the tears came. "Please."

"You wanna die," Meredith said, confirming.

"I wanna die. I wanna die."

"Let's do it," said Meredith, slamming the gas pedal to the floor. We went from twenty to eighty, fast.

"What's your fucking problem?" asked Valerie from the backseat.

"Jenifer wants to die, we'll die," said Meredith, hitting

ninety. When I said Meredith had the gift of go, I wasn't kidding. The world flew by.

"Oh my God!" Valerie screamed.

"Maybe I don't want to die," I said, but it was too late. Meredith swerved and we skidded sideways across the Major Deegan Expressway. We came to rest safely at the far edge of the right shoulder. It was quiet for a long time.

"We're fine," Valerie said.

"Are we?" said Meredith.

"Good. I'm good," I said.

"Good," said Meredith.

Valerie, Meredith, and I drove back to Harrison. We inhaled burnt rubber the whole way. It had burning sage beat by a mile. There wasn't much left for us to say. My sisters and I had almost violated our life's pact of eternal oneness on the Major Deegan, but we didn't, so there was no use talking about it.

After dinner Meredith turned off my light and I fell into a dream of the Century, the grand railroad train that once traveled back and forth from Chicago to New York. I loved that train. We had ridden it when we lived in Rock Island and my mother wanted to go home to New York to see her parents. Once, my mother took the five of us children into the dining car for breakfast. It was a very proper dining room with starched, pressed linens and fine silverware on the table, and the smell of freshly brewed coffee in the air.

My mother noticed the talent impresario Ted Mack at a table near us. He was reading his newspaper, minding his own business, but not for long. On the count of three, my mother made us stand and sing for Mr. Mack—"Take Me Out to the Ball Game"—as loud as we could. Ted Mack was very polite. He waited until we had finished singing, nodded his thanks, and left the dining car. He probably wanted to run. My dream that night took place on the Century, but it had a different ending. In my dream, when Ted Mack stood up at the end of our song, he didn't leave. He clapped for us. He stood and clapped a long time for a kid group that he honestly believed was going places.

"I'll see you very soon, Jenifer," he said, writing down his phone number for my mother.

"On the big show?" I asked.

"On the big show," he said.

I hit bottom that winter at Meredith's, but I was still dreaming of a better life. My sisters and I had survived the tornado of the absurd, but we remained hungry for answers. It occurred to us that we had been looking for answers everywhere *outside*. In our sadness and desperation, we had forgotten our own true strength. Then we stopped looking outside and turned our attentions in.

Chapter Six

IDIDN'T KNOW if I would ever have a baby, but I was sure starting to feel like one. Valerie and Meredith spent more and more time caring for me in Harrison. I couldn't stand up by myself for any length of time. They had to help me shower. Scott came up with his tools and an armload of lumber one weekend and built me a cedar bench for the shower so that I could be more independent. Meredith and Valerie grabbed me under each arm and helped me from my walker up over the lip of the shower stall toward the bench.

"God, I love the smell of wet cedar," Valerie said, trying to divert everyone's attention away from the fact that she and Meredith were dragging their totally naked sister to a bench in a shower.

"Is there any way you guys could close your eyes and do this?" I asked them.

"I think we've seen naked people before, Jenifer," said Meredith.

"Not each other," I said.

"Speak for yourself. I'm a total nudist," said Valerie, the liar. It felt okay when the water came, but I just couldn't—bathe—with my sisters there. They tried to respect my privacy: Meredith stood outside the shower staring straight ahead like a butler holding a bottle of shampoo, while Valerie washed me with a soapy washcloth, pretending not to.

"Do you smell the cedar?" Valerie asked.

"I smell the cedar," I said.

"It's enough with the cedar," said the butler, rolling her eyes.

I really hated asking my sisters for certain hygiene-related help. They had their own children to take care of. I had heard that you could call Medicaid for assistance with these things, so I did, and Memory came. Memory was my first home health aide. She didn't know anything about ALS.

"You have a car accident, honey?" she asked, coming toward the bed.

"You're the nurse?" I said, peering at her from over the edge of my comforter.

"That's me, Memory," she said, smiling. Memory was right up there with the giant and the maverick in her grasp of ALS. At least she had a pleasant smile. Memory had pretty gold rims around her front teeth.

"Your sister says you want to take a shower," she said.

"Yes, but I have ALS."

"I have a car accident one time."

"Yeah, well, I didn't, okay?" I said.

"Still you want a shower, honey," said Memory. "Trust Memory."

It was a relief when Memory took over, although it was totally humiliating being dressed and showered by a complete stranger. In my view, a woman should only ever have to utter the words "Can you get this button?" to a romantic prospect. The last time I'd said it was to Jeff Sherin, the best kisser on this green earth, bar none, whom I'd wanted to give me a hand—in a hurry—with my Anne Klein evening dress. But I had to hand it to Memory. She made a concerted effort to know me and my needs. She turned death-defying acts of grooming into predictable routine.

"Upsy, little daisy, and away we go," she'd say, standing next to my bed with my walker and our handy new travel pack of toiletries. Memory and I had gotten showering down to a science.

In bed at night, I started thinking less about skeletons and more about what Dr. Rothstein had said. He had told me my motor neurons were dying and they'd never be replaced. He'd said there was no medicine and to max out my credit cards. How did doctors get away with it? Doctors were supposed to make you well. I started taking the whole thing personally—and politically. I felt that my country had let me and millions of sick people down. If you had ALS, Alzheimer's, or Parkinson's, you weren't a citizen of the United States. You were strictly Third World. Why wasn't America declaring war on disease? It seemed to me we could be more efficient and aggressive in fighting brain disease, and not just by throwing money at it. Where was the game plan? Maybe a little violence would do the trick.

Violence was an option, I guessed, but for me it was just a Band-Aid. When Valerie was applying to college, it had dawned on her that waitressing wasn't going to cover her tuition. Our father had left us with nothing emotionally—the financial reality had never occurred to us. Valerie was right. We had no savings. We were forced to move out of Trilarch. Alison had already taken out gargantuan bank loans for her sophomore year at Brandeis, and my mother had just entered the workforce. She was selling advertising space for the local yellow pages. Alison, Valerie . . . how would any of us get through college?

"We'll find the money," I had promised Valerie as she paced the kitchen of our new house on Fenimore Drive one Sunday.

"Bastard," she said, opening the refrigerator and emptying its contents on the counter: cartons of eggs and a couple cans of Tab. "Help me with this."

"What are you doing?" asked Meredith as we gathered the eggs and Tab.

"Let's go," said Valerie. Before we knew it, Meredith and I were in the backseat of the Vega, speeding on Route 287 toward my father's new house in Armonk. My father was living there with his new wife, the reporter, and her children. Valerie pulled up to the curb near their house and cut the engine.

"When I say go, start throwing and don't stop," Valerie said. Valerie hadn't taught me the art of bombs for nothing. Meredith and I loaded up on eggs. My adrenaline pumped. *And five, six, seven, eight—*

"Go." We tore out of the car and up the driveway. Valerie launched the first eggs rapid-fire, hitting my father's new car.

Meredith flung eggs at the house. "Big, fat idiot!" she shouted.

I threw the bombs of my life, hitting my father's front door with one egg, two eggs, three bull's-eyes in a row. "Big fat idiot!" I shouted.

"Let's get the hell out of here!" screamed Valerie. We ran to the car, fell in, and tore away, hooting like marines all the way home.

"I've gotten a disturbing call from the Harrison police," said my mother, later that morning, as we sat debriefing in the kitchen. "Your father's wife has registered a complaint—something about eggs, desecration, and daughters."

"That bitch ain't seen nothin' yet," Valerie said, swilling a can of Tab.

"I believe you'd get farther faster, Valerie, if you refrained from speaking like a truck driver," my mother said. And she left the room. My sisters and I cried laughing.

But after the Tab ran dry, I felt dissatisfied. Egg

throwing wasn't my way, ultimately. Neither was violence. Messing up my father's new house with eggs had
been thrilling in the moment. But if I could grow up loving, working my hardest from morning until night, and
protecting my family—all the things my father hadn't
done—well, that would be my statement. I never saw my
father again. I grew to accept that his leaving was good
for everyone. It made me a much more responsible person. I felt proud taking responsibility for my own actions.
Pride, I realized, was the ultimate revenge.

I felt very responsible and mature—very nonviolent—
picking out my first wheelchair. Did I want to throw
eggs at every neurologist from here to Tibet? Yes, but
that wasn't going to get me anywhere. If I wanted to get
anywhere, I was going to need some wheels. Dr.
Rowland's nurse referred me to Homecare Solutions, a
store in White Plains. It was a Wal-Mart for the elderly,
disabled, and dying. The salesman took Valerie,
Meredith, and me on a tour of the wheelchair showroom.
It was a nightmare version of my grandpa Rosenberg's
University Chevrolet showroom in the Bronx, where my
sisters and I had hopped in and out of '68 Novas and
Corvettes just off the assembly line. We would fake-
drive to exotic locations.

"Where may I drop you, madam?" Valerie, my chauffeur, would ask.

"Hollywood Boulevard, please," I would say, sliding

into the backseat of a brand-new, gray-blue Monte Carlo. "I'm late."

"Right away, madam," Valerie would say, and we'd drive in place until lunch, when my grandfather would take us for grilled cheese sandwiches and egg creams at our favorite soda fountain off University Avenue.

It's a seller's market when you're dying. Our salesman was nice enough, but those chairs were gonna run us. The sheer scope of wheelchairs for sale was staggering, with one uglier and more expensive than the next.

"This is the Breezy," said the salesman, stepping back from one of his bestselling manual models. "Have a seat," he said, holding the chair for me. Sitting in a wheelchair for the first time was terrifying. There was a point-of-no-return permanence about it.

"So?" asked Meredith. I was in a state of shock.

"Do you like it?" asked Valerie. "Or, I should say, do you hate it less than you hate the other ones?"

"I think I'm a dead duck," I said.

"Maybe she wants more independence," suggested the salesman, hopping on an electric cart and riding it toward me. "Try the Jazzy." He looked like an idiot. There was no way I was going out in that thing.

"If you wanna spend a little more, there's always the Celebrity," he said. The Celebrity was displayed rotating on an Astroturf pedestal, basking in its own private spotlight. I had always dreamed of celebrity, but the possibility of experiencing it in wheelchair form made me want to run out of the store. It was bad enough being in a wheelchair. Why did they have to give them these names?

"Who comes up with these names?" I asked the salesman.

"It ain't Elizabeth Browning," said Valerie, folding up my new Breezy and putting it into Meredith's car.

I was heading toward a new acceptance. I was ready to use my walker, my wheelchair, whatever it took, to get me where I wanted to go. I wanted to go to new places. I was ready to work.

"What stinks?" asked Jake, coming home from kindergarten one day.

"Memory's fish," said Meredith, who had given over the kitchen to Memory during weekdays. The smell of Memory's daily fish fries was enough to knock you over. It made us long for a whiff of wet cedar. Who knew you could cook with that much oil at that high a heat and not burn down the house?

"Mommy, I think I'm a vegetarian," declared Jake right then and there. Thanks in large part to Memory, which they say works in strange ways, Jake became our family's healthiest eater—fruits, vegetables, and grains, all the way.

"You want fish, Jenifer?" Memory asked over the sound of boiling oil.

"No, really, you eat it." I said, pumping my wheels toward the dining room. My Breezy and I joined Meredith,

Valerie, and my friend Julianne Hoffenberg around the dining room table. It was a week before Thanksgiving and they were talking menu. Meredith had invited Julianne and Geoffrey to join us for Thanksgiving dinner.

"What should I bring, Mer?" asked Julianne, who had worked beside me at Naked Angels. I called her "Jules."

"Yourself," said Meredith, engrossed in her shopping list.

"Well, I'm gonna bring *something,*" Jules said.

"Bring me some medicine, why don't you," I said.

"Okay," said Jules. I had been somewhat of a mentor to Julianne. She had become a dear friend. She always aimed to please. "Seriously—what if *we* find the medicine?"

"Great," I said. Willis had told me that he and his friends had dug for medicine for me in the sandbox at Washington Square Park. Maybe Julianne wanted to dig in the park with Willis. They'd probably find medicine faster than Dr. Rothstein.

"Jules has a point," Valerie said.

"She does," said Meredith. "I mean, we couldn't do much worse than anyone else."

"There's enough brain power out there—enough raw intelligence. But no one's working *together,*" said Valerie.

"Or working efficiently," said Meredith.

"Maybe we could make them work together—" said Valerie.

"And meet deadlines," Meredith continued. "I mean, what happens to us when *we* don't meet deadlines?"

"Fired," I said.

"Fired," said Jules.

"They fire your ass," Meredith said.

"These doctors need to collaborate like we did at Naked Angels, don't you think, Jen?" said Jules.

"I'm thinking," I said. "I'm thinking." It was a big Andy Hardy moment. Gathered around the pre-Thanksgiving table, it occurred to us that we kids could do better. We could bring our business skills to bear on science, which seemed so all over the place. Effective management skills were effective management skills. We possessed those skills in spades. Heck, I'd produced plays before—why not a cure for ALS?

"Let's put on a show," I said. "Seriously, you guys, we could raise money—and use it to leverage these doctors to work harder," I said.

"This is what we do—we lock the smartest scientists in a room, and put a gun to their heads until they come up with a plan of action, kind of like the Manhattan Project," said Valerie. I didn't know what that was. "They invented the atom bomb fast. There's precedent here. We created the atom bomb. Why not medicine for ALS? We could call it . . . the A.L.S. Project."

"That sucks," said Meredith.

"How about Project A.L.S.?" suggested Jules.

"Project A.L.S. . . . Project A.L.S. . . . Hmmm, I like that," I said.

We all did. We got to work. I went back to my room to call friends in the business that might be willing to help. We decided to inaugurate Project A.L.S. with a star-studded fund-raiser in New York. We had two aims: educate people and raise the first bribe money for our Manhattan Project researchers.

I called Ben Stiller. He and I had worked together at Naked Angels, but our association went further back. His sister, Amy, and I had been friends as girls. I'd attended Anne Meara and Jerry Stiller's legendary New Year's parties since my teens. Amy, our friend Vicki, Ben, and I had made our own kind of music at those parties. We were like the junior brat pack within the senior one.

"I'm there, Jen," said Ben. "Name the time and place." Ben agreed to host our first event. Project A.L.S. was in business.

Our first office was my room in Meredith's house, where Jules, Meredith, and I worked the phones. We made lists and files. We took risks asking corporations to sponsor the event and celebrities to participate in it. Jules was brilliant at production. She called her old vendors and got commitments of goods and services at a discount. Meredith said our goal should be putting on a great show for no money and walking away with plenty of it. She crunched numbers while I called Kristen Johnston, another colleague of mine, an Emmy Award–winning actress from *3rd Rock from the Sun,* who agreed to join Ben as our cohost. Forget Valerie. She turned into that girl from *Poltergeist.* She went into the light of her computer and didn't come out. She continued researching the research relentlessly and set up first appointments with scientists at Harvard, Columbia, and Johns Hopkins.

"I don't know why you girls are starting something new," said Dr. Rowland as Valerie, Meredith, and I sat in his office. "There are too many organizations as it is."

"Don't worry, Bud, I won't embarrass you," I said. It was going to be hard convincing Bud or anyone else that Project A.L.S. was going to make major changes. ALS research had been chugging along for two hundred years, and no one else had found anything. Project A.L.S. decided to worry about the critics later. We had too much work to do. The first order of business was asking Bud Rowland to act as our research advisor. He accepted.

A harsh winter gave way to glorious spring. Acceptance of my own mortality had led to the birth of Project A.L.S. and an opportunity for me to work hard again. Meredith's house overflowed with activity. Valerie and Julianne worked the phones. My friends Geoff and Michael ran up Krispy Kremes from the city. I never saw Meredith without a calculator. Her baby was due in two weeks.

"Jenny, the First Lady of the city of New York wants to meet you," said Sue, a dear friend who had jumped in right away to help. Sue was close with Donna Hanover, then the wife of New York mayor Rudolph Giuliani. I knew of Donna as an actress, a journalist, and an activist. She was intrigued by Sue's description of Project A.L.S. Donna and I hit it off right away. She offered to give Project A.L.S. a press conference at Gracie Mansion before our event, and she invited me to speak at it. I asked

Donna if I could sit next to my friend, colleague, and for-
mer sit-ups partner, the elegant Billy Baldwin, on the
dais. I knew from experience that the press was more
likely to show up when and where famous actors did. My
sweet Billy. If the Estess sisters and the Baldwin brothers
ever did a remake of *Seven Brides for Seven Brothers,* I
know which brother I'd pick.

Meredith couldn't come to the press conference. She
would be giving birth that day. Her doctor wanted to
induce labor and had no other availability. I missed
Meredith the morning of the press conference in more
ways than one. I was afraid that without her, I wouldn't
look my best. It was my big return to New York. With all
due respect, Memory didn't quite cut it in the fashion-
and beauty-advice department. I was going to be seeing
my friends for the first time in my wheelchair. I wanted
to look pretty and as confident as possible. My mother put
on my lipstick. That was an adventure. Memory laid out
a couple of horrific outfits at first, but we eventually settled on a decent pair of slacks and my burgundy blouse. I
could still blow-dry my hair, but I had to use two hands.

"I have to use two hands now," I said.

"So did Chrissie Evert," my mother said. "And look
how far she went." I really missed Meredith.

The first person I saw when I rolled in to Gracie
Mansion was my friend Martha. I took her in. She took
me in. We both started crying. "You look so beautiful,"
she said and hugged me for a long time. My fear of being
seen by the people I'd hidden away from in Harrison dis-

appeared. I talked to a lot of people. Then it was time to start. My mother sat at the back of the room. Valerie watched from the side of the dais. Billy wheeled me to my place next to him. He kissed me.

"You look great, Jen," he said. I spoke into the microphone. As I described that first twitch in my leg that Meredith had noticed, I saw the reporters in the audience look down at their legs. When I talked about making ALS a topic of national concern, I saw them write in their notebooks. My speech was effective. Of course—Valerie had written it. After the press conference, Billy wheeled me to a terrace off the south side of Gracie Mansion. The sun was on us, brilliant and warm. I looked downtown toward NYU Medical Center, where Meredith and James, who had just been born healthy at nine pounds, were resting comfortably. No drugs for Meredith. She had pushed a few times and that was it. "Done," as my most efficient sister is fond of saying.

I was done with the better part of the scariest year of my life. Project A.L.S. had developed almost instant momentum. My sisters, friends, and I had worked our butts off. I was working harder than ever in my life. Our inaugural benefit at the old dance hall Roseland, in New York's theater district, was a great success. It raised hundreds of thousands of dollars for research. Valerie, Meredith, and Jules were in the car the next day, delivering research grants to scientists whom Valerie had found.

The night at Roseland was spectacular. Nancy Jarecki, who was the first person to join the Project A.L.S. board of directors, and her husband, Andrew, greeted me at the entry ramp. I was so nervous to go in there in my wheel-chair. I was scared that people I hadn't seen would view me as a marked woman whose days were numbered. But Meredith and I got me looking quite good. The Jareckis coached me up the ramp and inside. Everyone was so happy to see me and so gracious, my nerves went away. The food was good. The wine was good. The messages from the stage were direct and moving. People gave me checks for Project A.L.S. It was my wedding, basically. As a producer, I had always prided myself on creating entertainment that had emotional impact. Otherwise, why bother? I think that Project A.L.S. achieved that its first time out. The eight hundred people in attendance that night became a family that would grow—and work together—to change the course of a river.

It was time for me to leave Meredith's house. Watching baby James on my bed, I was sure of it. I looked at James's round face and his smiling eyes. He was a tiny swaddled Buddha.

"What would your best day look like, James?" I asked him. "Your very best day . . ." He looked past me to the tree outside my window. The haunted tree from last winter was now covered with buds and new leaves. It was bursting with life.

"Is that what you want, James?" I said. James just stared at the tree, vibrating. "Well, we'll just have to work for it. You and me," I said, touching his cheek with my hand, which felt weaker than I wished.

The Hulberts were in the driveway to see me off: Meredith with her arms around Jake and Jane, baby James sleeping in his stroller, Peter crying, and Memory. As Valerie and I loaded into the car, I was sad and excited to be returning to New York City, this time to a wheelchair-accessible building near Valerie's house in Greenwich Village. I smelled summer in the air. It was my favorite season. In a few weeks an acquaintance of mine named Reed would be coming to New York from Los Angeles, where he lived and worked as an actor. I don't know why, but I'd picked up the phone early on to tell Reed that I had ALS. I didn't know Reed that well. He was handsome. He had made me feel safe the times we'd been together in health. So I called him.

Reed had already visited me once at Meredith's house. I don't know how to describe it: There was something about the way he put his hands around my waist that I loved. There was undeniable energy between our bodies. It was weird being on a walker and being attracted to a guy at the same time, but at the end of the day, anatomy was anatomy. Reed and I had the anatomy thing going.

My life, in its unconventional way, was falling into place. I had a new job, Project A.L.S., a new apartment in a doorman building in Greenwich Village, and a cute guy coming into town to see me for the summer. As I waved good-bye to the Statue of Liberty, and to all she'd taken in, I looked forward to my New York homecoming.

Chapter Seven

M Y NEW APARTMENT in New York was on West
Twelfth Street in an elevator building. I was an
uptown girl by nature, but I felt safer being downtown,
only a few blocks away from Valerie. If there was an
emergency, she could get to me in minutes. I was right
across the street from St. Vincent's Hospital. Everyone
said how great that was, though there wasn't much St.
Vincent's could do for me. Ambulance sirens screamed
day and night: *Dying people stuck in traffic.* That took
some getting used to.

I found that with every move, I had less to unpack.
Jeans and sweaters, winter coats, anything made out of
wool or leather or layers, was too much for my body to
bear. Gravity was pulling me down, so I shed my clothing. I brought only a couple of boxes with me from
Meredith's to Twelfth Street, lightweight sweatpants and
T-shirts mostly, and photographs in frames. I bought a
new electric queen bed that, as advertised on TV, made

sitting up and lying down easier. Through the Visiting Nurse Service, Medicaid sent over my new home health aide, Lorna Cofield, a quiet, caring woman my age who worked weekdays. Twelfth Street had wide doorways for my wheelchair and a roll-in shower. For a few hours each day it got good sun.

With the success of the first Project A.L.S. benefit behind me, as scientists dug deeper in the sandbox to find medicine, I got sunnier. My friends insisted on taking me out in my wheelchair for walks in the scenic West Village. One time Geoffrey took his eye off the road— someone caught his eye on Perry Street—and he ran me right into a tree. Geoff, Jules, Bradley, Jace—they all played down the perils of going out for an ice cream cone. No one wanted to admit that taking me out in the wheelchair was a life-or-death proposition. Our gang didn't know from wheelchairs. We knew from the Keystone Kops. That's who we were, pushing me over cobblestones and hauling me up the warped curbs of Greenwich Village.

I started staying inside, where I was still able to use my walker for short trips to the bathroom, living room, and kitchen. The more I stayed in, the more my mind wandered to Reed, who was due in town from L.A. any day. Why was I so excited to see Reed? He and I had met years earlier in the theater program at New York University, and again at Naked Angels. He was one of those guys who camped out occasionally on the periphery of my vision. He wasn't a focus. I always assumed that Reed wouldn't like me *that way*. So I never bothered liking him *that way*. I never invested in Reed. But we definitely hit it off as friends. When Reed and I were out in a group at dinner, we would always manage to find each other around the table. When he stayed with me at my Seventy-first Street apartment a few times on his way through New York, we did some serious laughing. Reed and I actually made love one night in Nantucket. We snuck into a hotel room during the Nantucket Film Festival, which I had helped to produce. It was a great time, but in the morning he wore sunglasses to breakfast. It was like *Invasion of the Body Snatchers*. He pretended not to know me. From then on, Reed always made a point of telling me about this or that girlfriend. It was never simply Natalie or Caitlin. It was always "my girlfriend Natalie" this, or "this girl I've been seeing, Caitlin" that.

I didn't know if Reed was coming to New York that summer just to see me, but I decided not to question it. He was planning to stay at his friends Billy and Maura's town house on Charles Street. I figured if I saw him once in a while that would be great; if not, great. Mostly I was excited to see the guy because I sensed he knew how to protect me physically. He had strong hands and perfectly chiseled . . . everything. Reed knew the human body, all right. When he wasn't acting, Reed was running or swimming. He was like a large dog. Give him a yard and a ball and he was happy. Reed's body was a textbook illustration of health and vitality. Mine was another story, although I still thought I looked pretty decent.

"Seriously, how do I look?" I asked Meredith and Valerie, who were hanging out on the floor in my new room one day.

"Better than you have in a year," said Meredith.

"What if Reed hates the wheelchair?" I asked.

"Screw him," said Meredith.

"He can kiss my ass," said Valerie. My sisters and I were beyond protective of one another in love matters. If two sensed that the other was about to have her heart broken, they closed around her like the Mob. *You come near my sister, I'll kill you.* It was a bit over the top. Valerie and Meredith never thought I had the best taste in men. They accused me of going for the cheesecake. Granted, I was attracted to cheesecake in many forms. When it came to romance, I definitely had my own style. I started with dessert. I wanted a husband and children like my sisters, but my pursuit of the dream wasn't as linear as theirs. Starting from childhood, I had made my way in love as in so many other things, without the benefit of a road map.

I was married once for a brief time to Robert Redford. We wed in an ultraprivate ceremony in my bedroom with the door closed. I was thirteen and he was an eight-by-ten glossy taped to the wall over my bed. As I touched his golden hair, I vowed to have and to hold—

"Through sickness and in health," he said. We were already finishing each other's sentences. I had met Robert Redford at the Rye Ridge Cinema, where I saw *The Way*

We Were seventeen times during an extended run. My mother, who was just divorced from my father, was glad to drop me off for afternoons alone at the movies.

"Don't worry about me, Mommy," I called after her. She was already halfway to the light. They all knew me at Rye Ridge.

"The regular, Jenifer?" asked the smiling woman in a paper hat.

"Plus a Junior Mints today, Josie, please," I said.

"So, how is . . . he?" she asked, topping off my popcorn with an extra shot of butter.

"I tell you, Josie, the man is a lifesaver," I said, walking toward my love in the dark. Who is as gorgeous as Robert Redford playing Hubbell Gardner in *The Way We Were*? Nobody. The man knew his way around a carrot stick. His crunching wasn't annoying like other people's. His smile, his hair, his fisherman's sweater—

"It seems like all you care about is what a guy looks like," said Valerie.

"Is that so bad?" I asked.

"If he's a horrible person it is."

"Hubbell isn't horrible. He's beautiful."

"He's a character in a movie," Valerie said. People were always so quick to judge. That's why Hubbell and I cut off from the world. I was fascinated by Hubbell's relationship in the movie with Barbra Streisand. This time, Barbra played Katie Morosky, an outspoken Jewish girl who wanted Hubbell more than life. Katie bent over backward cooking Hubbell the perfect steaks, ironing the kinks out of her hair, getting him a writing job. She made all the first moves. But Hubbell never loved Katie *that way*. He thought she pushed too hard, the ultimate turnoff for a guy like him. Life according to Hubbell wasn't about pushing. Pushing was messy and desperate. *Wait a second* . . . I pushed a lot. I was a big pusher from way back. Wasn't that the way to get things done? *Hmmm,* I thought, *does a girl push or should she be craftier?* What was that phrase . . . *feminine wiles?* Instead of calling Hubbell, maybe she waits for him to call her once in a while. Dial the phone or sit by it? It was a disturbing dilemma for a girl.

"Another Junior Mints, please." I was back at the concessions stand.

"Is there trouble in paradise?" asked Josie. She was getting on my nerves.

"We're fine, thank you," I said curtly. In the end, of course, I'd married too young. I realized I needed seasoning, other experiences. Robert Redford stared straight ahead unblinkingly when I told him I thought we should see other people. I don't know if he believed me, but I swore to return someday, if only to run my fingers through his hair one last time.

After the breakup, I had a hard time getting started with boys. My best friend, Nancy, was so frustrated with me that she started pimping me out at parties. She made me sit next to her in the circle for Spin the Bottle. I wanted to run out of the room. I kept thinking that when the bottle came to me, the guy would say, "Ewww, I'm not kissing her." Those boys weren't even kissing anyway. They were banging their heads against the girls' heads. A few boys had their mouths open. I couldn't figure out where they were going with that. The girls didn't seem to be enjoying themselves at all. My ex had spoiled me. I decided to hold out. I was looking for a certain skill level, a certain carrot crunching.

"You need to be kissed," said Nancy, who was obsessed with getting me my seven minutes in heaven. Nancy loved Timmy Kelly, the David Cassidy of our grade. He was adorable and funny and a good athlete. Nancy told me to shadow her. She said if I did exactly as she did in her cunning pursuit of Timmy, I'd land myself a whopper, too. My life changed abruptly when Timmy took me aside and told me that he was in love with me. It was a real eye-opener. The most popular boy in the school loved me. I loved Timmy, too, but not *that way*. Maybe my loyalty to Nancy prevented it, but there was no way I was getting involved with Tim. But just knowing he loved me made all the difference during a confused time. I fit in suddenly, and without all the muss and fuss of adolescent groping. Timmy landed on his feet, too. He and Nancy got together for about seven minutes. Everyone was happy.

"There's a new guy in tenth grade," said Valerie one day as we sat in the cafeteria cutting class. I was more interested in my Linden's butter crunch cookies than just about anything. I knew what to expect from those cookies.

"Listen to me," said Valerie. "He's a man in a boy's body." And in he walked, on cue. Michael Dwyer, a tanned boy in clogs wearing overalls without a shirt. He was a teddy bear with muscles, a great head of curly brown hair, and granny glasses. My heart stopped. I had to figure out the best way to meet Michael Dwyer. I made Valerie drive by his house at night.

"This is so idiotic," said Valerie, turning in to Michael's narrow winding driveway. As we reached the house, a floodlight flashed on.

"Oh my God, he sees us!" I screamed, and Valerie slammed into reverse. This went on for about a week.

"And the point of this exercise would be?" asked Valerie, who would've rather been watching the Knicks game.

"I don't know. I don't know what to do," I whimpered.

Valerie did. "Why don't you go up to him and start talking." After all the hemming and hawing, it made sense. Talking—it was a rational strategy somewhere between tackling and teasing, somewhere between Streisand's Katie Morosky and a Harrison High School cheerleader. It worked. My first real kiss was with Michael Dwyer, when I was fourteen and sitting cross-legged on the front stoop of my house. He leaned down and took my face in his hands. *Soft,* I remember thinking. Then he put his lips on mine. *Warm,* I remember thinking. The guy had tremendous potential—carrot-crunching quotient, off the charts. As we kissed I felt the cold of the cement through my jeans. *Right,* I remember thinking.

Maybe on some level I knew I'd die young and that if I was going to have a long-term relationship I'd better get down to it. Michael and I fell in love and were together for five years. As products of broken homes, we slid through the regulatory cracks. No curfews or drug testing for us. Michael and I were free to love each other like mad. It was poetry. Picture a slightly less attractive Romeo and Juliet.

Michael's mother lived in a rambling old house in Katonah, a pretty suburb north of Harrison, where he and I stayed for long, snowy weekends in the winter. The Katonah house became ours. Michael and I grocery shopped and argued politics. We wore sweaters together. We socialized as a couple, were known as a couple, and lived in my mind as a couple. Thanks to advice from my sister Alison, who at seventeen became the youngest student in the history of Brandeis University to serve as president of the Student Sexuality Information Service, I approached sex responsibly. I came of age with my diaphragm in my purse.

"You were born older," Valerie said. I felt that Michael was born older. We were a woman and a man living the best years of our lives together a little ahead of schedule. When Michael and I decided to make it official, his father took a sudden, passionate interest in me. Michael's father liked me, but he felt that Michael was too young for marriage. I guess he had sway. The day after a rip-roaring fight, I saw Michael's yellow Beetle convertible parked in my neighbor's driveway. My neighbor was younger than I was. She had a boring face and legs for days. I went crazy on Michael. He went away.

For most of my early twenties I was like an Italian widow. I swore off men for mourning over Michael. He had been my life. Now he was gone. There were others in time: Eddie, Tico, Phil. Each hinted to me of love the way it ought to be. But no one was meant for me, not in the way Michael had been in his prime. Meredith and Peter were meant for each other. That's what I wanted, and I was going to wait for it. Jeff came close. Jeff Sherin, a stranger in a tuxedo, walked into my crowd's annual New Year's Eve party, and the whole room fell in love with him. I was the only one who got to go home with him. I was free in my Anne Klein dress and my Donna Karan tights. I was free out of my dress and tights. Nights with Jeff were some of the best, but when the sun rose on us I never felt relaxed with him. Jeff wanted me to join him in his parents' hot tub. I wasn't the jump-in-the-Jacuzzi type. I wanted us to take our time over coffee and current events. Besides, I wanted to lose a few pounds before I got into anyone's tub.

"When will I see you again?" I couldn't resist asking Jeff.

"When you see me again," he said, which meant minutes, months, I never knew. Then Jeff disappeared completely. A friend told me he'd married and divorced a Singapore model. Jeff and I saw each other a few times in the years after that. He was a wolf, I realized, one of those men who kisses and talks to you and makes love to you so expertly and gently and generously that you think he's in love with you. I still had vague notions of taming the wolf and of our ending up together down the line. Then Jeff died. His young heart gave out on a snowy mountain. I cried hysterically when I heard. I wanted to be with him. A month later, I was diagnosed with ALS. My friend Kathie said that my diagnosis was Jeff summoning me to him.

"I like this bed, Jen," said Reed, lying next to me on my new shift-o-matic, sending us up and down with the clicker. He had stopped at my new apartment straight from the airport.

"Thank God," I said, and Reed laughed hysterically. Reed and I had a verbal chemistry. He provided the setup, something benign and flat as a wheat field like "I like this bed." And I came back with sarcasm, the murder weapon. I could slay Reed with the slightest intonation. Reed and I were very Nick and Nora, platonic, of course.

Reed arrived at my bedside in June looking perfectly tanned and coiffed. (I think that Freud would have been proud of me. Every single guy I ever pretended to date, dated, or thought of dating had amazing hair, which probably meant that I wasn't trying to marry my father.) Reed wore his army fatigue shorts just so. His T-shirt fit him perfectly, and his sandals revealed flawless, tanned toes.

"The guy's a doll," Valerie said. There was something Ken-dollish about Reed, but for my sisters, I think that his perfect looks were an easy target. Outwardly, they were defensive of me, but in their heart of hearts they were praying for Reed and me to fall in love and get married, and for Reed's love to be the medicine that would make me better. As far as I was concerned, Reed presented a safe way out of the house. He certainly looked safe— and dangerous.

"Lorna!" I shouted.

"Coming," said Lorna, who helped me dress, prepare meals, and turn in bed when I couldn't, which was more often now. Lorna was my lady-in-waiting.

"What do you think of this lip gloss?" I asked.

"It's nice," said Lorna. To Lorna everything was nice, good, or fine. When my sisters asked Lorna how I was doing, it was always, "She's real good."

"What do you think of Reed?" I asked.

"He's good, real nice," said Lorna.

Lorna got a big dose of Reed and me that summer. Reed was either on his way out for a shower back at Billy and Maura's—he was very Lady Macbeth with the washing—or on his way in with a take-out dinner and movies for us to watch. Reed came and went with the wind. That summer, I was along for the ride. Reed was a Zen master with the wheelchair and my body. He knew how to nudge the chair, lift it, carry it. I never felt bumps. We never derailed. With Reed at my back, it was all smooth sailing. He made me forget I was sick.

Our first night out he pushed me along Seventh Avenue. Women stared at me. What was someone their age and outwardly healthy-looking doing in a wheelchair? And was it contagious?

"Such a beautiful night—my husband and I couldn't resist," I said to one. "We just had a baby boy. Give her a cigar, honey."

"I'm all out," said Reed.

"Then let's haul out," I said, and we took off.

"Congratulations!" the woman called after us.

Reed and I pushed westward to the edge of the Hudson River. The black water lapped up against Manhattan. Our hair blew in the breeze.

"When will I see you again?" I asked.

"Tomorrow," Reed said. We saw each other day and night for two months. Reed and I tread where few New Yorkers had dared—the edges of sidewalks, the steepest subway stairs—all with me in the wheelchair. An actor who was also a terrific photographer, Reed was determined that we see the city through a convex lens, starting with Fellini. He pulled out his perfectly folded movie listing with Fellini's *Nights of Cabiria* at eight o'clock neatly circled. I hoped he was in the mood to push the wheelchair for about six hours, because it was playing way uptown at Lincoln Center Plaza.

"We're taking the bus, Jenny," he said. I didn't do mass transit when I was healthy. It seemed crazy to start now. "Do it for me," Reed said. The idea of doing it for him suddenly appealed to me. The guy had sky blue eyes. I took a deep breath and prepared to board my first Sixth Avenue local. The bus driver opened his doors, took one look at me in the chair, and closed the doors, but not before Reed forced them open again. He got right up into the driver's face. Within minutes I was strapped into my appointed cranny on the bus with Reed next to me. I think that we both felt triumphant. We got to the movie theater early. Reed got me onto a stone bench in the courtyard of Lincoln Plaza. To look at us then, we were a normal man and woman—stunning, I might add—just waiting to see a movie. Later, in our theater seats, Reed fed me Cadbury cookies. His crunching was positively Redfordesque. People walked past us in the aisles. I smiled at them; they smiled at us. I felt so proud. Thanks to Reed's persistence, I was back in the land of the living.

At the end of the night, Reed transferred me from my wheelchair to my bed. It was our first time. The transfer with Reed was unlike any physical experience I'd had. My friends, Lorna, my sisters, no one knew how to get me out of the chair without a major planning discussion first. Reed knew instinctively. As he held me tight around my waist and pulled me up and toward him, I felt beautiful. He looked pretty good, too. We were heart-to-heart, as close as two people could be in a thrilling, wordless dance over to the bed. From that night on I didn't want to let go of Reed. I was deep into my Summer of

Love, my last chance to have love with a man. My heart rushed to get everything in.

"Lorna."

"Coming," said Lorna, balancing my wicker basket full of cosmetics with my morning coffee. Lorna and I had gotten used to getting ready for Reed. We'd already changed outfits five times that day. Meredith had bought me some new shirts, and Lorna and I were plowing through a bag of them. The drawstring pants worked, finally, with a scoop neck, light blue tee. It was a look—not my first choice—but one I was determined to perfect for Reed and me. Meredith also threw in some Annick Goutal, a fragrance that drove me wild. Lorna doused me. I looked pretty damned good, if I do say so, in the scoop neck and my new lipstick from Chanel, a gossamer shade. I couldn't wait to see Reed.

"I like me a man, Lorna," I said.

"That feeling is a fine feeling," she said. "It's a real good feeling." I kicked into high gear. I called my old friends in the beauty business. They generously made house calls—hair color and cut, manicure and pedicure. My friend Martha gave me dangling earrings. I was back. Reed arrived smelling like soap. We were ready to go.

"I'll pray for you," said Lorna, a deeply religious woman.

"That may not be necessary," I said, feeling especially confident, as Reed rolled me out the front door. We went downtown to the World Trade Center, where small out-door concerts during the weekdays were a well-kept secret. A few Wall Streeters lingered during their lunch as the music started. It was jazz. I got the beat, baby, instantly. So did Reed. He lifted me onto his lap in the chair, and he wheeled us back and forth to the music. I leaned back into him and wrapped my arms around his neck. The sun was warm on my face. People stared at us dancing in the wheelchair. I think they saw my love.

Women worry about a pimple. Women worry about ten extra pounds, or whether they're smart enough or pretty enough to be loved. I used to have the same worries. They kept me very busy. Then I got ALS. Leave it to me. It took a deathly disease for me to realize that if I wanted to love someone I could, with no restrictions, no matter how I looked or who I was. Love was my right as a woman, my responsibility, my manifest destiny! Love was my best thing. I was a Love Girl. I wanted to love Reed with everything I had in the time that I had. It didn't matter if he felt the same way. My love was my love. I was ready to pursue it.

My heart may have been ready for love, but my body wasn't. Each first experience with Reed was clouded by a ghostly awareness that it was my last—my last dinner with him in a restaurant, my last time swimming with him in the pool on East Houston Street, my last dance. I felt a Donna Summer song coming on: "It's my last chance for romance tonight." For the first time in my adult life I was ready for a thousand sunsets, but I had time for only one. It happened on the roof of Billy and Maura's brownstone. Somehow Reed had gotten me in the wheelchair to the top of the steep narrow stairway. When he got us to the roof, Reed paced like a proud father, his T-shirt drenched in sweet-smelling sweat. Getting me around New York had become Reed's extreme sport. We drank Absolut and cranberry juice as the sun went down.

"Do you see the Empire State Building, Jenny?" he asked, taking pictures. It was kind of hard to miss. I took it all in, especially the subtler Village skyline. To the east I thought I saw Valerie's house. I pictured Valerie and Scott and Willis safe inside. I loved them so much. Up the river to the north I saw Meredith and the Hulbert house, which had been a harbor to me during my most difficult days. I looked to the river. How many more times would I see it? I was getting quite a buzz on from the cocktails. I needed that kind of help saying good-bye to the skyline. *Good-bye, New York.*

"Watch the sun and the water," said Reed. It was the end of another New York day. The huge burning sun, hot and tired from work, was about to cool off in the Hudson, or so we thought. Right before the sun fell into the water, it disappeared behind New Jersey. That was surprising.

"I love you, Reed," I said.

"I love you, Jenny."

The summer was already ending. Reed's duffel was halfway packed. He asked my advice about flights back to Los Angeles.

"It's July," I said. He already had one foot out the door. Valerie put a couples' dinner together. Meredith and Peter, Scott and Valerie, and Reed and I met at Bar Pitti, for wine and pasta and sautéed spinach. From there, Reed and I were going to the theater. We all sat in the middle of the restaurant, three sisters in love. How Reed got me to the heart of that crowded restaurant I don't remember. How he got me to the theater at the height of the theater rush I'll never know. Or down into the subway, or surfing an escalator at the Loews Cineplex, or into the basement of the Village Vanguard. I can close my eyes and see Reed on Rollerblades pushing Willis and me fast, faster, mind-blowingly fast down to the ends of the city. The man knew my body. He knew how to be with me at a time when no one else did. Reed knew my needs and he anticipated every one of them.

The Summer of Love was *my* love story. My feelings drove the narrative. But let's face it, I wanted Reed to return my love in every way, shape, and form. I wanted us to get married and for him to see me through to the end. Maybe I pushed too hard, for Reed showed not the slightest hint of changing his plans. He would return to Los Angeles as scheduled on Labor Day weekend. On one of our last nights together we sprawled out on my bed watching *The Silence of the Lambs*. Reed had his back to me. It was a scary movie. I longed for him to hold me, not in a treacherous stairwell or on top of the Empire State Building, but in the way a man holds a woman when they're watching a scary movie. I wanted to reach out for

Reed. But I couldn't reach him—I literally couldn't reach out with my arms to hold him. That was even scarier.

The day Reed left was my last day of walking on earth. It was a Sunday. He was on my bed watching a preseason football game. I was contemplating getting to the bathroom using my walker. The scene was a fast-forward glimpse of what Reed and I would be as an elderly couple.

"I don't think I can walk anymore," I said.

"Don't be ridiculous," Reed said. He was eating a sandwich and talking to the quarterback. "Just use the walker."

I didn't want to disappoint him. I wanted to keep walking. I wanted to walk to Los Angeles. I pulled myself up in bed. I knew I was going down before I took my first step, my last ever. "Reed . . ." I crashed to the floor. Reed was at my side. He held me.

"I'm sorry, Jenny," he said. "I'm so sorry." What was he sorry for? I had done things with Reed that summer that I never would have done as a healthy person.

Reed and I transferred one last time. Lorna and I had dressed my bed in satin sheets and a cashmere blanket for the occasion. I sat next to my bed in the wheelchair. Reed faced me. For us, the transfer had become an art form. My friend Martha said she learned everything she needed to know about love between a man and woman from watching Reed and me transfer that summer. Reed put his arms around me and lifted me to him. I smelled his soapy smell. I cried hot tears into his neck. For those weeks Reed and I had been as close as two people could be. As I held my face against his, I wanted to kiss him. *My last kiss.* I could have, but I wasn't quite ready to say good-bye to kissing, or to Reed. That one I'd save for later. We held each other for a long time, rocking. Then he put me down onto the bed. He sat looking at me, then staring off Hubbell, my Hubbell. I had sworn to return to him, if only to run my fingers through his hair one last time. I ran my fingers through Reed's hair. He was crying. He picked up his duffel, promised to call, and left for the airport.

About a week later, photos arrived in the mail. Reed had captured the essence of the summer with his camera. There were beautiful pictures of New York, of my family and me. In my favorite, I am sitting on the grass with the World Trade Center behind me. I am smiling and looking healthy, looking at Reed.

Chapter Eight

IT WOULD HAVE BEEN NICE if Reed had gotten down on his knees at the end of the Summer of Love and asked me to marry him, but he didn't. He *so* didn't. When he sashayed out my room for the airport, my heart shattered. I started dreaming about him. I didn't want to dream about Reed. I wanted to throw fruit at his head. But every time I closed my eyes, I saw us racing down Seventh Avenue or eating cookies with Fellini. I spent the first few weeks after he left crying into my pillow and talking my sisters' ears off about Reed, Reed, my Reed.

"This is so sick," said Meredith as I talked compulsively about Reed in his shorts and sandals. "I hate those sandals," she said.

"Awww, don't be mean to my baby with his little shoes," I said. I was out of control. In my heart I knew that no one would touch me again the way Reed had. What does a woman do when a man breaks her heart? One plots revenge. Another vows never to make the same mistake again. I ate candy. Late one night, after a nightmare starring Reed in truly unattractive sunglasses, I called on my bedside stash of Rolos, the genius chocolate and caramel candy that gave me solace. But reaching for midnight snacks wasn't so easy for me anymore. I was horizontal. My outstretched fingers were inches from the Rolos and victory. I channeled Reed for one final push. *Oh, Reed.* It didn't work out—as I lunged for the Rolos, I fell out of bed. I fell and I couldn't get up. I had two options: stay on the floor until morning when Lorna arrived, or somehow get to the phone and call for help. *Stupid Rolos . . . Hey, wait a minute,* I thought. *Rolos. Roll . . . over. Roll over.* With everything I had, I rolled once, twice, toward the phone, which was up on my nightstand next to the candy. I pulled the cord as hard as I could, the phone came crashing down to the floor, and I dialed for help. Within minutes, Valerie and my friend Michael were picking me up and dusting me off.

"Such ingenuity, Jen," said Michael, who is the hardest-working actor I know.

Ingenuity was part of it. I had good ideas. But my true salvation after that heartbreaking summer with Reed was my other great love in life, work. Reaching, rolling, falling, fighting, holding on, speaking out—hard work had been my salvation as a girl and it was my only hope now. I had said it in health, and I was saying it again, louder: Love and work are the most important things in life. Without love and work, a woman is a shambles. She's a Rolos-eating mess.

Just as I had known that Reed was my last chance at romance, I believed that Project A.L.S. was my last stop on the work train. I was using everything I had to make Project A.L.S. unique and compelling. I turned away from Reed and focused like a laser on the work. My self-doubt and the occasional fears of failure that had plagued my earlier efforts in the working world were gone. Fueled by the lessons of my past and facing what was very possibly my last chance to work, I became my most efficient self. Along with my sisters and friends, Project A.L.S. and I began a methodical, thrilling, epic chase for robbers who were stealing lives. I couldn't run after the robbers anymore. But I knew that with ingenuity and hard work, I might catch them.

My sisters and I were already building Project A.L.S. from shitdust—you'll excuse the French—into a young, respected force against disease. That's because we were taking on the problem of ALS for the first time as a team, as a family. Scientists thought that our "family approach" was novel—or new. I didn't think it was new. I thought it was as old as the hills. It was absolutely essential that scientists and doctors and corporate leaders and government officials work together to make sick people better. I also believed that if we continued executing our plan, Project A.L.S. could become to disease research what MGM had been to the movie musical. We could become the best at what we did.

I had always wanted to be the best at something. When I was seven, I could do the Hula Hoop better than anyone in my family. Even my mother was impressed. Since then, I had made an effort to try to do my best at every job. It wasn't always easy. I got fired a couple of times. But at the end of the day, I could always say I had worked—that I had put in a good, honest day of work. I could always say I'd earned my night's sleep.

As my body weakened, though, I wondered if I was going to have enough energy left to push Project A.L.S. over the top. The company was off to a great start, but we needed to grow. In order to grow right, we needed to impose a structure on ourselves. I thought for a long time about whether I could say yes when Valerie, Meredith, and Jules offered me the job of Project A.L.S. CEO. It took me about two seconds. I finally had my own company. Project A.L.S. was in the business of finding medicine for an incurable disease, or, as our closest advisors might have said, accomplishing the impossible. I believed that my sisters and I were as qualified as anyone to make that happen.

My best work had always come from passion and love. As a senior at Harrison High School, I was already building a respectable résumé. After two years at Clover Donuts, I was promoted to head grill girl. I flipped donuts *and* burgers. I had a steady boyfriend. That definitely qualified as work. On the home front, my mother got her first paying job. After she moved us into a smaller house in Harrison, she started selling gigantic ones. Of course, my mother thrived as a real estate broker. Better than anyone, she understood a family's dream of living in a modern-day castle. My mother's dream had come true for about five minutes with Trilarch. She was helping her clients hold on to their dreams for a little longer. I felt proud that my mother was finally doing what she'd spent her best years motivating my father to do.

At a certain point, my working in the food business was like an alcoholic tending bar. Most of what I earned at Clover or Butler Brothers delicatessen was canceled out by my tendency to eat the profits. Help was on the way. My humanities teacher, Mr. Toppo, approached me one day after class to say he thought I should audition for the Declamation Contest, an annual event at Harrison High School that featured students acting out monologues. The contest was sponsored by the local outpost of the American Legion and was judged by a panel of Legionnaires, teachers, and independent experts in diction and public speaking. I auditioned for the Declamation Contest and was selected as one of the final six contestants.

I fell in love with acting the moment I tried it. I also fell in love with Mr. Toppo. I was seventeen at the time—he was about 110. This was to become a pattern—my falling head over heels for any man I worked with intimately, regardless of his age, availability, or sexual orientation. Mr. Toppo and I worked for weeks on my monologue, which I had chosen from Ingmar Bergman's *Face to Face,* a dark, complex portrait of a psychiatrist's descent into a nervous breakdown. At seventeen, I found that I liked exploring the dark side of the human psyche. There was something familiar about it. Mr. Toppo seemed stunned by my openness in rehearsal. He said I had a great instrument. Finally, on the day of the contest, I couldn't hold myself back.

"Mr. Toppo . . . I think I'm falling in love with you," I said.

"If this were another time and place, perhaps," he said, correcting papers.

"Mr. Toppo?"

"Yes, Jenny."

"I can't tell if I'm good at acting because I'm in love with you or because I'm just good at acting," I said.

"Tonight is only the beginning for you, Jenny," he said. "Good luck out there."

I was out of my body the night of the Declamation Contest. The auditorium was filled with an audience in the hundreds, the judges, and most of all my love for what I was doing. I took the stage as Bergman's embattled protagonist wearing a diaphanous nightgown, uninhibited and completely free. I ripped through my monologue, giving it my simplest, most honest interpretation. The crowd went wild. I won. When the head of the American Legion stood up to announce my name as the winner, Valerie and Meredith shouted and whooped in the aisles. Mr. Toppo stood at the fire exit with his arms folded, quietly nodding. Backstage, Mrs. Oberstein, the elegant school speech therapist, approached me weeping, thanking me for my performance. Mrs. Landau, the empress of all English teachers, who had preferred teaching my more studious sisters and had taken much less notice of me, pulled me aside.

"You became a woman tonight," she said, looking into my eyes. I felt humbled and gracious. I shook hands and kissed people congratulating me as Mr. Toppo, my first acting mentor, graciously stepped back into the shadows. I wasn't in love with him anymore, but I loved him.

I think I was born to act. Unfortunately, I was also born to stop myself from acting. For some reason, I didn't trust my love for it. Acting felt too good or something. I just didn't understand how anything in life could come so easily. There had to be a catch. Almost immediately after my emancipation onstage in the Declamation Contest, self-doubt came a-calling. Self-doubt was a problem I'd inherited in part from my mother and one that I would fight for years. I was fine working at jobs I didn't love. But when it came to the pursuit of my deepest passions, I felt inhibited sometimes and unworthy. My father had been born with a sense of entitlement. He believed he had the right to walk into a restaurant and change its menu. In my attempt to separate myself from him, I think I might have gone too far in the other direction. Sometimes I didn't feel entitled to my dreams at all.

I went on to study acting at New York University, but self-doubt seeped into most every performance and my every opportunity to work. I would become physically sick from stage fright. I'd call Valerie from backstage moments before an entrance, telling her I couldn't go on.

"What's the worst that could happen?" Valerie asked.

"Die," I said, choking on fear.

"You're afraid to live is what," she said. "Just get out there and pretend you don't give a shit." Okay, so she wasn't Stella Adler. But Valerie convinced me to get out onstage and do my job. "Just complete," she said. I managed to make my mark onstage on a few glorious occasions.

Valerie had always fascinated me. She was my older sister. She had been a parent to Meredith and me. Valerie had never missed a single one of my performances, including dress rehearsals. After college, she was right there loving me through difficult patches, praising my successes. No one believed in me more than Valerie. She believed I saw things first, knew them first—well, you know the drill. But you didn't want to ask Valerie what *she* was working on.

"Crap," she'd say. "That's what." My sister Valerie clearly understood the importance of work. She had worked her ass off from the time she was fifteen. She was never without a job. Hers was one puzzling résumé. Valerie had studied English in college. She wanted to be a writer. But for five years, ten years, fifteen years after graduation, she didn't write.

"I can't write," she'd say. "My writing is like an alien's writing." Okay. I realized I had my work cut out for me. Valerie had been my life's guide, my first one. She put me through the basic training that had solidified my values, my habits, and my work ethic. But when Valerie hit her twenties, boy, did she ever need a kick in the pants from Meredith and me, her own graduating class.

Valerie and I were always creative soul mates. Meredith didn't understand our mind-bending, never-ending quandaries. Meredith figured if you wanted to do something, you did it all day, as simple as that. She had gone to college and immediately to graduate school. She had pursued jobs in fashion merchandising because that's what Meredith wanted. Boom. Done. Valerie and I, on the other hand, constantly questioned our motives. We talked endlessly on the phone and over coffee and into the night about the creative process. Not that we had many creations in process—we just liked to put our minds to the issues of art and creativity.

It was thanks to Valerie's patience over the years that I was eventually able to accept the fact that work brings disappointments along with success, that work isn't a bed of donuts. I learned that work was always going to be a mixed bag, no matter the job. But Valerie herself wasn't interested in mixed bags. She felt that unless she wrote like Tennessee Williams, she should be stripped of the right to write.

"We already have a Tennessee Williams," I told her. I wanted Valerie to know that we needed one of her, too. Just because I wasn't Meryl Streep didn't mean I shouldn't act. Also, if acting was going to give me so much to think about and *so little to do,* maybe I should consider changing jobs. I was learning maturity. I was learning a give-and-take. Valerie taught me that give-and-take, but she'd for-

gotten to teach herself. Now I mentored her. I tried anyway. She wrote five short plays.

"They pretty much suck," said Valerie, handing me
the scripts. They were fine plays. They needed work, but
the grain of goodness was right there on the page.

"Do you think you can work on these?" I asked.
Valerie worked on the plays and saw them performed.

"So, what did you think?" I asked, after a roomful of
people clapped for her plays.

"I think I need work," she said.

"Yes, isn't that great? There's so much to do," I said.
Valerie was starting to know that everything—every
painting, kitchen cabinet, chocolate soufflé, could use
some improving. The point of the game was to stay in it.
You had to be in it to win it. Valerie and I taught each
other that taking risks was difficult and necessary.

After college, my friends from the NYU Theater Department started a company called Naked Angels. Out of
curiosity, I went over to The Space on Seventeenth Street,
the company's new home, and I didn't leave for years.
Acting was giving me a tough way to go. I tried working
through my fears at Naked Angels by taking a part in the
Joseph Heller play *We Bombed in New Haven*. *We Bombed
on Seventeenth Street* was more like it. I wasn't that good
in the play. But, truth be told, I wasn't that bad, either.
More than anything, acting had just become a source of
annoyance and frustration. I made a conscious decision to

walk away from it for a while. I could always come back if I wanted to. In the meantime, I figured, I'd be a producer. Valerie said it: I'd always had a knack for seeing the big picture.

Naked Angels was a great place to cut your teeth if you were a fledgling actor, playwright, director, or stage designer. My fellow company members included so many talented artists: Marisa Tomei, Rob Morrow, Kenneth Lonergan, Jon Robin Baitz, Gina Gershon, Nicole Burdette . . . but there was no one running the joint. My friend Merrill and I built up the office from zero. Merrill had some great ideas. He showed me the importance of a dynamic board of directors. He and I were careful to build a board that would give back to the company: raising money, bringing ideas, and donating in-kind services. John Kennedy was on the board. He provided me with many in-kind services. First—let's just put this on the table—the man was insanely elegant and gorgeous. I had just never seen such grace in a human being before. Another Naked Angels board member, Martha McCully—also insanely gorgeous—and I would sit at meetings, bewitched by John. His was an uncommon beauty. John was a mentor—I learned a lot about self-discipline working side by side with him. He was a master at letting things roll off his back. I tried to copy him.

If I may be so bold, I'd say Naked Angels eventually became *the* place to be for emerging artists and audiences. We never advertised our plays, but orchestrated a word of mouth that gave Naked Angels a cache, an air of mystery, a certain underground glamour. Naked Angels became the hottest ticket in town, not only because we were savvy in our "branding" but because we nurtured gifted artists in their formative years. We promoted art in progress—an excellent product, in my opinion.

I remember watching the Academy Awards as a girl and wondering what producers did. I could picture actors and directors and costume designers at work—but it was hard visualizing a producer. This is what I did as a producer: I took productions of plays under my wing. I worked every aspect of productions, from getting corporate backing to working with writers on scripts to advising directors, listening to actors, and selling tickets. If the heat wasn't coming up through the pipes, that was me. The producer was responsible for soup through nuts. If Jacqueline Kennedy Onassis was stopping by the office to talk to me about John and his love for the theater, I had to make myself available. (Talking with Mrs. Kennedy Onassis was one of the great honors of my life.) During the day, I worked hand in hand with the company and the board to ensure that The Space was a nurturing place. At night, I worked the schmooze, dining and dishing and drumming up excitement for Naked Angels. I got people to fall in love with Naked Angels and give us things. Some nights thinking about work, I was too excited to sleep. I was crazy in love with my job. For my five years as producing director, Naked Angels previewed the next generation of talent—my generation.

When it came to my career, I was never a pampered

pooch. I was never groomed to run the family business. I had made my own way, so that one day I could offer my son or daughter or niece or nephew the chance to inherit and improve upon what I had built. I was a student in business from the start. Mentors had been a key to my learning, so I sought them out aggressively. I picked up the phone and called Sue, Kathie, Simon, John, Michael, and others whom I'd admired from afar and wanted to learn from and asked if I could meet with them. I was always afraid that the person on the other end of the phone would think, *Who is this little pisher calling me?* But I called anyway. It was never easy picking up the phone. None of it was easy, come to think of it—the nerves, the cold calling, making meetings with strangers—but all of it was necessary.

"I just want to do a good job, Simon," I said, during my job interview with him. I was interviewing for the position of account executive at the public relations firm Baker Winokur Ryder. I didn't really know what public relations was, but after Naked Angels, I just had to start earning a decent wage for myself. "I just want to do a good job," I said again. Simon got a big kick out of my wide-eyed earnestness—he was a bit taken aback by it. I was never too good at business-speak—you know, that buttoned-down way of presenting your case. My strategy was going into an office and speaking my heart. It wasn't necessarily a winning strategy, but it did win me the chance to roll up my sleeves and get started with Simon.

I spent the money as soon as I got it. That was just my way. Making more money, I figured I could spend more on my sisters, my mother, my future husband—wherever he was hiding—and my nieces and nephews. Simon Halls gave me a chance to earn more—so I could share more. I was confident about my prospects. Almost as soon as I started at Baker Winokur Ryder, I hatched my next plan— the big kahuna. I had always wanted to produce movies. I dreamed of bringing high-quality entertainment to millions of people, and there were two people I wanted to work with in making it happen—Valerie and Meredith. With valuable experience under my belt, I hunkered down for hard work in my glorious thirties. I looked forward to a life sentence of hard labor. Then I got sick.

One of my favorite plays was *The Three Sisters* by Anton Chekhov. In one scene the three sisters sit around the samovar, talking about their lives. They are still hurting from the death of their beloved father a year before. Although the sisters are full of dreams, they feel directionless. Then they remember—*the work*. It is a revelation for them, a forgotten treasure. Yes, the sisters are heartbroken. Yes, their lives haven't worked out as planned. But suddenly they are invigorated by the following realization: They still have work to do. It was the same with Valerie, Meredith, and me. When all seemed lost, when Reed walked out my door, and illness prevented me from doing the same, my sisters and I still had *the work*. ALS wasn't our first choice of work, but it was what we were dealt.

There wasn't time to stop and worry about whether our work was pretty or a masterpiece or inspiring. As a bunch of nonscientists, we didn't stop to worry if we were allowed to challenge science and medicine. Fear and self-doubt had become luxuries my sisters and I couldn't afford. We had a lot of work to do, and we didn't have much time. My sisters and I became the Charlie's Angels of ALS.

I was the stay-at-home Angel, working phones from my bed. My ALS was moving into my arms and torso, so going out on the town wasn't an option anymore. It was too dangerous. Even with a custom-made wheelchair, I had trouble holding my body up. One wrong move, one uneven curb, and I would have gone flying off the chair. I couldn't rely on my muscles to keep me safe and upright. Living on my bed for most of the day worked in one respect: I got a lot done. It's not like I could hop up and go out for lunch. My fingers were getting less nimble. It was hard dialing friends just to talk. I worked more than I had ever worked before, because I couldn't get away from it. I used a headset while Lorna dialed for me. For conference calls, Jules, Meredith, and Valerie gathered around my speakerphone. I learned a million ways to say the same thing: The state of ALS was unacceptable. Project A.L.S. was going to change it. Can you help us?

As I romanced corporate America from my bed, Meredith and Valerie worked over the scientists to come up with new, more aggressive approaches to research. These doctors, who seemed nice enough, hadn't managed to come up with medicine for ALS in two hundred years. Why was that, exactly? We knew they could do better— we set out to help them do their best work and hold them accountable. My sisters, Jules, and I had been held accountable in every job we'd ever had. Either we completed a task by the stated deadline or we were fired. We taught scientists about deadlines: I was talking *dead*lines. Project A.L.S. led with cattle prods. I think that the researchers and doctors appreciated our directness.

While I worked at home, Angels Valerie and Meredith hit the road, recruiting the most gifted, creative scientists—many of whom had never thought about ALS before—and molding them into a dream team. Project A.L.S. funded this dream team on the condition that the players work together, share data, meet regularly, and beat deadlines. Traditionally, scientific research was done in isolation—the guy in Podunk worked on his project, the gal in Hodunk worked at her project, and they never met to share their findings or to discuss how their projects might connect to the larger body of ALS research. The traditional work model seemed totally ludicrous to us. Scientists worked as competitors, not collaborators. Crazy! Teams, armies, communities, a houseful of sisters, a country as one—every major championship, war, and consensus that America had won, it had won through some form of togetherness. We founded Project A.L.S. on the same notion—that ALS would be solved not by

brilliant individuals working in isolation, but by commit-
ted, aggressive teams of researchers working together. It
was the American way. It was our way. It was the only
way we were going to win this thing.

One of our first breaks came in early 1999, when Valerie
got a hot tip about a renegade scientist and neurologist
from Children's Hospital at Harvard University. Evan
Snyder was using stem cells to make mice that had been
genetically engineered to shake and wobble stop shaking
and wobbling. Valerie and Meredith went up to Dr.
Snyder's lab and pinned him against the wall—kidding.
They asked him if he thought that stem cells might also
help people who wobble with ALS, or other degenerative
brain diseases or injuries. Dr. Snyder said he thought that
they could, and a new idea was born—using stem cells to
understand and treat ALS.

Over the next two years, Project A.L.S. created a
world-leading consortium including stem cell experts,
molecular biologists, ALS clinicians, and others to test different kinds of stem cells in laboratory models of ALS. In
one set of experiments, Douglas Kerr and John Gearhart
of Johns Hopkins University showed that stem cells
helped paralyzed rats walk again. A group of scientists led
by Hynek Wichterle and Thomas Jessell of Columbia
University and the Howard Hughes Medical Institute
showed that stem cells could be *nudged* to become brand-
new motor neurons, the cells that die in ALS. Both

groundbreaking studies were formed, funded, and over-seen by Project A.L.S. We knew how to nudge, too. I loved that Dr. Jeff Rothstein was on our team now. The same man who had told me my motor neurons were dying and they'd never be replaced was starting to show that stem cells might one day prove him wrong.

Work allowed me to take out my frustration over the fact that nothing had been done about ALS by doing something. Work was an outlet for my fear, too. My arms got weak so fast. My fingers started curling in. They reminded me of *The Wizard of Oz,* when the witch's feet curl up under Dorothy's house (for me, the scariest part of the movie). Soon I wouldn't be able to feed myself. I had a night nurse now, Karen Jack, who rubbed my feet and listened to my midnight confessions. Dishing with Karen became a ritual that I looked forward to. I noticed that my breathing was becoming ever so labored, which meant that my diaphragm, the flat muscle that expands and contracts the lungs, wasn't working as efficiently. With ALS, the writing was always on the wall. Each day I came across a clue telling me which part of my body was going to be destroyed next.

At the same time my body wiped out, my pride grew mightily. I marveled at Valerie's and Meredith's ability to go out into the world, challenge it, and bring home the kill. They worked with such grace, intelligence, and economy.

"I learned it all from you," Meredith said as she crunched numbers on my bed.

"I learned it all from you," I said.

"And I would be chopped liver," said Valerie, who became director of research for Project A.L.S. Listening to her talk to scientists on the phone made me feel hopeful. It took her about ten minutes to learn their language. She had mentored me; now she was motivating some of the world's greatest scientists to do better.

Build it and they will come. We did and they did. As Project A.L.S. made inroads, magazines and newspapers got interested. *The New York Times* and *People* ran stories about us. Then my friend Patricia Harrington introduced me to Katie Couric. One day, when Valerie and Meredith were down in Washington at a meeting with the Food and Drug Administration, Katie came to my bed. We talked and talked and talked. Outside there was a blizzard. As the snow piled up, Katie and I spent the whole day getting to know each other. I felt as if I'd known her before. No doubt, we would have been best friends as girls. She probably would have been as good if not better than I was at the Hula Hoop. I admired Katie's demand for journalistic excellence—she seemed to be a perfectionist like me. I totally fell in love with her soul. It was profoundly kind and kindred. Not to mention we were on the same page when it came to men. As single women (Katie had lost her beloved husband, Jay Monahan, to colorectal cancer), we both wondered about our chances of finding new love.

Soon after our meeting, Katie reported an in-depth segment about Project A.L.S. on the *Today* show. It elevated us to a whole new level. Our phones rang off the hooks. More corporate sponsorship followed—*InStyle* magazine, Bloomberg—and more researchers signed on. Valerie built a tight-knit research advisory board of universally respected scientists and administrators to guide us to our next level of discovery in the laboratory. Jules, Meredith, and I put together our board of directors, a downright remarkable group of friends, activists, and philanthropists. My sisters and I were on our way. We didn't know if we'd get there in the time of my life, but we swore to get there, to the mountaintop, where hard work, love, and determination foretold medicine for people who were dying.

My work for Project A.L.S. made me feel more entitled, though not in a selfish way. I was just so confident. I felt that I could do anything. I couldn't reach out literally anymore, but I wanted to keep reaching in every other way. Forget fear and self-doubt. If by some miracle I got better, I'd do a lot more acting. I'd ring Reed's doorbell and the doorbells of many men. I'd be uninhibited and free and confident. I pictured myself as a woman in health, running, not walking, toward what I wanted.

Chapter Nine

AFTER TWO YEARS living on Twelfth Street, I started calling my carpet "the food and beverage carpet." People spilled on it all the time. No one knew why. It was a phenomenon. If a friend came in to my room with a diet Coke, chances are she was going to spill it. Friends would say, "Oh my God, Jen, let me get some paper towels." And I'd say, "Please, please don't worry about it. This is the food and beverage carpet. Everyone's spilling." Even more mysterious . . . my ocean blue carpet appeared to absorb everything from beer to pasta, and it never stained or smelled.

"We should really get Stanley Steemer in here to clean this carpet," Meredith said, after knocking over one of her trademark iced teas.

"I don't think we need it, Mer," I said.

Aside from the food and beverage carpet, my bedroom was unremarkable, except for the photos covering every inch of my walls, bureau, and radiator. The faces of my

nieces and nephews made people stop in their tracks—
they were *that* beautiful. One of the most mesmerizing was
a close-up of Kate, Valerie's daughter, the latest addition. I
was never able to hold Kate in my arms by myself. When
Valerie brought her home from the hospital, she lay new-
born Kate in my lap and put my arms around the baby and
held us there. That was about the best we could do.

As my arms and hands became paralyzed, as my body
shut down, I was grateful to be able to commune with
photos of my friends. Some people look to crosses or the
Torah for inspiration. As I got sicker, I looked to photos
of my friends. Some were of my friends with me when I
was healthy, at parties, at the beach, in the good old days.
I couldn't believe how much my body had changed. I had
been a much prettier person than I remembered.

My friends showed up in person, too. Old and new
friends came to my bed. Before I got sick I was all over
New York. Nothing made me happier than throwing on
some jeans and catching a movie with Martha and
Merrill, or meeting my posse after work at the Odeon, a
Tribeca restaurant with great roast chicken and mashed
potatoes. Going out with friends wasn't always easy
breezy. There was a certain pressure that came along
with showing up at all the right places with all the right
people—and being *on*. What if *I* wasn't right—what if I
was *off*? Many nights I would have much rather stayed
home alone with a cake. But the more I challenged
myself to get out there socially, the more I began to relax
and enjoy myself.

Now I rarely left my bed, which after two years of constant use had become a whining, arthritic queen. Each time my nurses sent it up or down with the clicker it groaned with dissatisfaction. I remembered the early days of ALS, when Meredith and I dressed up my bed with fabulous sheets and comforters. Now we just couldn't be bothered. My nurses used a plain flat sheet to move me around. I had to be shifted constantly. I breathed easier lying on my side. Coughing was easier sitting up. On the millionth count-of-three, Lorna, Karen, or my new nurse, Juliet, would pull my sheet and me toward the closet or toward the window or toward the door or toward the wall, depending on whether I needed to breathe or cough or eat or sleep. They lifted and lowered my arms, legs, and trunk. They adjusted my hands and my head. My nurses were like hands on the deck of a ship in a never-ending storm. My bed and I were the ship that they steered and manipulated.

As I was being lifted, shifted, and rolled, I thought about my summer with Reed two years before. I had been much more mobile then. When Reed had held me that summer, I could hold him back. I had been able to absorb the insulting bumps and bruises that New York dished out to people in wheelchairs, but I couldn't cut it anymore. I missed my laugh a lot. Without laugh muscles, all I could muster now was a flat, forced "aaaaaa." I hated that sound. It was a real joke killer. A baby monitor was my latest piece of equipment. It became a lifesaver, as my once booming voice and laugh—my friends had always

140

said they knew exactly where I was sitting in a theater—disappeared. The baby monitor was my connection to my nurses in the living room.

The living room, also known as Project A.L.S. World Headquarters, was just beyond my door. During the week, our associate director, Nina Capelli, worked in the office as I worked on my bed in my room with my sliding door closed. First thing in the morning, I would hear Nina out there pleasantly answering the phone, "Project A.L.S," and our executive director Dana Kind, and producer Jonathan Burkhart strategizing for our next event, while Lorna and I were behind closed doors trying to get my head through a turtleneck. My lifestyle was less traditional than ever: I lived where I worked. I ate where I slept. I bathed on my bed. God knows I would have traded it all for a husband and a house with a normal carpet, but that wasn't my fate.

I saw the world from my bed. Lorna got me ready. She would sit me up in my black turtleneck and black cotton pants, cross my legs, and balance my hands on my knees. She'd prop me up all around with bean-filled pillows. I looked like a Buddha or a tepee. Then she'd slide the door open and my friends would come in. I can imagine how nervous people were to see me. They probably didn't know what to expect as time passed. But once my friends came to the bed, they didn't want to leave. I didn't want them to leave, either.

My friends were impressed with the food and beverage carpet. They loved my whole room. They said it was out of time, that it was a time machine. My friends said my room was sanctum sanctorum, a sacred place where they didn't feel judged. They said it was a spiritual spa where they could relax and let it all hang out. As their confessions flowed, my desire to listen to them grew stronger. I wanted to offer help where I could. I wanted to help so much. I had sleepover dates with Simon, four-hour lunches with Katie, business strategy sessions with Sue; all of it seemed out of time, as if my friends and I existed in a parallel place.

Martha McCully walking in to my room—there was a gift. My friend Martha looked more beautiful to me with each visit. Martha and I had shared a taste for the best things, always—beautiful people and restaurants, fabulous vacation spots. In health, Martha and I were weight-conscious to a fault. We wanted to lose ten pounds forever. That forever nagging feeling was so far away now. Talking on my bed, Martha and I felt more and more that we were a-okay, and that ten pounds would never separate us again from the lives we wanted. Martha brought over her new boyfriend to meet me. I felt like Judge Judy while they sat there holding hands and answering my pointed questions. I was so proud that Martha was in love, the most empowering feeling, but I wasn't totally sold on the guy. He was a little defensive. Plus, where were the flowers and candy? For Martha and me, romance was always a subject "to be continued." Focusing on how we could improve ourselves for *ourselves,* and not for our potential boyfriends, remained one of our biggest challenges.

I may not have been a whiz when it came to my love life, but friendship I knew. I had a knack for giving my friends dead-on romantic advice. It gave me joy sharing my best feelings about Martha *with* Martha, being Katie's bed spy, letting Caroline wrap me in the pale blue cashmere blanket that she had brought for me from Europe and hearing about her latest date.

I was always a big believer in family values. You'd be, too, if you had a family like mine. Friends were my family. I'd have toasted them right there on my bed: *To my friends—that family of mine* . . . but I couldn't hold a glass anymore. I probably would have spilled on my carpet anyway. After her piece about Project A.L.S. on *Today,* Katie came back to my bed with a new boom box for me and encouraged me to listen to music again. Thanks to Katie, Frank Sinatra was back in my life. In short order, Katie brought me another man, my new Sinatra. Rob Kaplan was Katie's friend, and he quickly became my brother. Rob and I bonded the moment we met. We talked about love, his upbringing in Kansas, and Project A.L.S. I learned the finer points of leadership and philanthropy on the bed with Rob. He and I covered territory in a hurry. Ours was a deep friendship in fast motion. We wanted to get everything in. Rob and I were busy people, but we always had time to check in with each other by phone. He had occasional questions about women. I had eternal questions about men. I was Rob's romance 4–1–1. He was my spiritual 9–1–1. Rob became my Sinatra, my brother, my husband, business mentor, and eternal friend. I don't know what Freud would have said about Rob and me, but I had stopped trying to please Freud a long time ago.

"You're an old fuddy-duddy," Valerie had told me when I was ten. "You're an old lady or something." Some saw a wisdom in my chubby face—a certain age, a knowing. My math teacher came to me for advice. So did kids in my class and their mothers. My own mother had taught me the master class in friendship: If I could help her, I could definitely help others. My mother and I confided in each other throughout her divorce, subsequent remarriage, and boyfriends.

"I don't have *boyfriends,*" my mother sneered.

"Okay, *man*friends," I said.

"I don't have manfriends. Men are fools, every last one of them," she hissed.

"With all due respect, Ma, you're never without one." I believe my mother loved men more than she loved herself—that was the biggest problem. Over coffee with the woman I idolized, I observed the many subtle ways in which brilliant, gifted, exotic women diminished themselves in relation to the world. Men did it, too. I wanted to stop the people I loved from doing this. From a young age, I had tried to save them.

"Who do you think you are, Holden Caulfield?" Valerie would say. "Why don't you mind your own business?" I have always felt that other people's business *was* my business.

When my mother fell head over heels, crazy in love with the man who became her second husband—I called him Number Two—I was forced to bring my A-game. It was really scary. After three dates with Number Two, my mother had already changed her smart wardrobe to all flouncy dresses; she had permed her hair and started talking in uncharacteristically girlish whispers. She was another person. It was like *The Stepford Wives*. Hey, I liked a good makeover as much as the next girl. But this was ridiculous.

"Isn't he an elegant creature?" my mother marvelled as we sat in the car watching Number Two exit the liquor store with a brown bag. "Watch how he *moves,* Jenifer. He's all about economy." He sure was. Number Two was so cheap, he and my mother took over Alison and Valerie's room after they got hitched, without even asking. The guy sure saved on rent.

My mother was definitely in love with Number Two. I was genuinely happy for her. I don't think she'd ever been in love with my father. But the price she paid! My mother gave Number Two the farm. The farm was all of her intelligence, her strengths, and her elegance. She projected it all onto him. *He* was the elegant one. It was hard staying patient with my mother sometimes. I told her she needed to look in the mirror. Then she would see her worth—and that perm had to go. When I was a girl, I had noticed a lot of girls and boys, and women and men, giving away the farm. It was epidemic. A lot of people looked to *the other* instead of looking inside for happiness.

It was like me buying a Rolls-Royce or a house in Malibu, expecting that those beautiful things would fill me up, or like Dorothy searching for fulfillment in Oz when her heart was home—inside of her—the whole time.

I advised my mother. I advised my friends. They filled empty spaces for me, too. After my father left, Valerie, Meredith, and I rebuilt our family with friends. We all shared the same ones. We made our house home to them after school. We broke bread with our friends. We went away for weekends with them. At fifteen, Valerie was de facto head of our growing household. Through living with friends, my sisters and I learned the value of one big, happy family.

It wasn't all rosy. After my father left, the holidays were especially depressing. When I was a girl, my mother had always made such a big production of our Jewish Christmas. I was Eloise at The Plaza. Christmas was my absolute favorite time of the year. I think I believed in Santa until I was thirteen. On Christmas mornings, my sisters and I would rush downstairs to find that the living room had been magically transformed into a winter wonderland with hills of gifts in shiny wrapping. I still looked forward to Christmas, but the tenor of it changed after my father left. My mother definitely wasn't up for magic making. I was worried about her.

Then Donna and Elsa came in. Donna and Elsa were more Valerie's friends, but Meredith and I looked up to them so much. Valerie met Donna on the Harrison Huskies girls' basketball team. Valerie played forward;

Donna was their outstanding point guard. Elsa was Donna's best friend, a college student who watched games from the stands with her sunglasses on. Elsa was so cool she could have been Fonzie's sister. Donna and Elsa became Valerie's parents. Elsa picked Valerie up after school in a cool brown Firebird; Donna cooked Italian dinners for her. We all felt safe around Elsa and Donna.

One Christmas Eve during high school I was struck by a sad silence. Our usual friends had gone home to be with their real families for the night, and the house felt cold and hollow. My mother was alone in her room with the door closed. Valerie, Meredith, and I just sat there as the afternoon got darker and darker. Then Elsa and Donna busted through the front door, carrying a huge Christmas tree. We'd never had a Christmas tree before.

"Please, Mommy, can't we have a tree?" I remember asking my mother when I was little.

"Jews don't have trees," she'd say. Well, they did now.

As Donna and Elsa hoisted the tree inside, our house filled with the smell of pine.

"Take a deep breath," I said, filling my chest with rarefied air. Meredith and I roamed around the house just taking it all in. Then we all decorated the tree together, with lights and ornaments that Donna and Elsa had brought. When we were finished, my mother came down the stairs, took one look at our tree, and started to cry.

"How beautiful . . . how beautiful," she kept repeating, as she wept in Donna's and Elsa's arms. For some very lucky people, family is a fixed entity: one loving mother and one loving father supporting their healthy, happy children, and they all live to be 150. But for me, family was friends. It was growing and ever changing—it could always be bigger. Elsa and Donna bringing over the tree was an act of faith that I will never forget—it marked a renewal of my own faith. I ended up feeling very religious that Christmas. Family, in its ever changing shapes and sizes, was my religion of choice.

My friends had helped me to come of age in high school. My friends put Project A.L.S. on the map. As I navigated my third year of ALS on the bed, friends kept coming on board to make our mission a reality. It was my friends' belief that our growing family would wipe ALS from the face of the earth. The world's leading researchers, who worked intensely with Valerie, became our father figures. Corporate leaders—people like Stephanie George of *InStyle* magazine—became sisters and brothers to Meredith as she honed our business plan. I made a new friend in Senator Arlen Specter, United States Senator from Pennsylvania, who invited me on behalf of Project A.L.S. to come to Washington to testify before his and Senator Tom Harkin's Labor, Health and Human Services Subcommittee. Senators Specter and Harkin had coauthored a controversial bill proposing federal funding for stem cell research, and they wanted a panel of knowledgeable Americans to answer the subcommittee's questions and concerns on the matter. Thanks to

Project A.L.S. and others, scientific research had already provided intriguing evidence that stem cells might ultimately save ten million people dying with ALS, Alzheimer's, Parkinson's disease, and life-threatening disorders of the spine and brain like multiple sclerosis and spinal cord injury. We thought that the government should see about saving ten million Americans right away. Project A.L.S. was going to Capitol Hill.

The Amtrak trip to Washington was a blast. Reed flew in from Los Angeles just for the occasion. We reserved a whole train car for the Project A.L.S. entourage. There were Valerie and Meredith, board members, friends, Reed, my nurses, a lot of candy going around, the press, and me rehearsing my remarks. Later that morning, I had the honor of testifying alongside Christopher Reeve, my shining knight in the fight for increased and concerted government support for stem cell and scientific research. In my speech I talked about the American Dream that I had had as a girl growing up. I told the subcommittee that ALS was a national disaster that needed the government's attention immediately. I spoke of Project A.L.S.'s hard-earned laboratory results with stem cells. My goal was to inform the gentlemen and -women of the Senate. I think I succeeded. A few months later, Senator Specter invited me to testify again. This time I spoke with Chris, and more new friends, Mary Tyler Moore and Michael J. Fox. We had all joined the fight. When it was my turn to speak, I reminded the subcommittee that people blind-sided by life-threatening illnesses and injuries had the same American Dream as everyone else. I felt Chris, Mary, and Michael's support as I ended my remarks: *Each day I speak from inside my body, which has now become a prison. I am still here and dreaming of an America that will protect our rights to life, liberty, and the pursuit of happiness for all.* Applause followed. Afterward, Senator Specter thanked me for coming. I told him I hoped to see him again soon.

During the train ride home from my initial subcommittee appearance, as towns flew by, I thought about Project A.L.S. and the progress my friends and I were making. I thought about my friends, the incredible artists who had pledged their ongoing support for Project A.L.S.: Ben Stiller, Katie Couric, Melissa Etheridge, Julianna Margulies, Edie Falco, Caroline Rhea, Sheryl Crow, Rob Morrow, Marisa Tomei, Kristen Johnston, Camryn Manheim, Sarah Jessica Parker, Matthew Broderick, Gina Gershon, Billy Baldwin, Laura San Giacomo, Helen Hunt, and the list goes on and on. I thought about my friends, the thousands of Americans who were sending in generous donations and letters of encouragement. I thought about my friends Katie and Martha, who gave me hope for womankind. I thought about my friends the Wertliebs, the Abramsons, the McGraths, the Decters, and the Kaufmans, families from all over the country fighting with us to save their children from the devastation of ALS. I thought about my friend the courageous young Katherine Moore of Rocky Hill, Tennessee, whose father had died from ALS, and who had asked her friends to donate to Project A.L.S. instead of giving her presents for her tenth birthday. I looked forward to receiving Katherine's thoughtful cards. Maybe one would be waiting for me when I got home. The train kept going. I had a lot to look forward to reaction to our first trip to the Senate, working on the next Project A.L.S. public service campaign, and my sleepover. Simon and I were supposed to have a sleepover that night back on the bed. Simon gave great dish.

I could feel us—my sisters, friends, and I were a bullet train speeding toward the answers to unanswerable questions. Scientists were unearthing stunning facts about stem cells, cells that were somehow attracted to areas of injury, migrated to those areas, and fixed what was broken there. What a miracle, the miracle of life. It occurred to me that the people I loved were like those cells. Me, too. We were attracted to areas of injury. We migrated to those areas. We did what we had to do for each other. Project A.L.S. was moving fast and efficiently. It was my dream company, a train that wouldn't be stopped. Could stem cells or any of the other potential therapies that Project A.L.S. researchers were working on come in time for me?

Sometimes I would dream about getting better. There I'd be sitting around a huge family table with thousands of friends celebrating. We'd pass around roast turkey, mashed potatoes, and platters of perfect chocolate cake. We'd eat the meal that made America strong.

"Please pass the potatoes, Senator Specter," I'd say to the gentleman to my right.

"Passing you the potatoes would be my distinct pleasure, Miss Estess," Senator Specter would reply, as our
dinner went on until dawn.

Once when I woke up from the dream, I noticed that
my breathing had become even more labored. I was
working too hard for each breath, straining my neck
muscles to help me. My neurologist, Dr. Rowland, came
for a house call. Sitting on the bed, he confirmed that my
breathing had been affected—my diaphragm muscle and
my chest muscles had grown weak. He prescribed a bi-
pap, a truly unattractive ventilator that would force air
into my lungs and suck it out through my nose, force it in
and suck it out—in an unending cycle of assisted breathing. When the bi-pap was delivered to my door, Valerie,
Meredith, and I cried.

Karen helped me put the mask on. The bi-pap mask
was like a second, even bigger nose. It was a gawky plastic triangle that formed an airtight seal against my face. It
wasn't a good look for me. A huge hose connected me
and my mask to the breathing machine on my nightstand. Basically, I was now wearing a vacuum cleaner to
stay alive. The bi-pap scared me. Even more than paralysis, the bi-pap represented a point of no return. Deep
inside I knew that the medicine Project A.L.S. was fighting for probably wouldn't come in time for me, but that
my friends and I had to keep working. We had children
to fight for.

Valerie slept next to me my first night using the bi-
pap. It took us a long, long time, but eventually Karen

came in with blankets and we got some sleep. The sun, Valerie, and I rose the next morning after my first successful night of using a machine to breathe. The bi-pap was a setback, but not an insurmountable one, as the next day reminded me.

The day after my first night with a ventilator was a banner day for Project A.L.S. Valerie came in excited about a phone call that she had just received from Fred Gage, a researcher at the Salk Institute in La Jolla, California, who was working with Project A.L.S. on stem cells. Dr. Gage told Valerie about a new discovery in his lab. It wasn't stem cells, but a new *gene therapy* that he thought might be effective in ALS. Did Project A.L.S. want to fund a pilot experiment? As Valerie shared the good news with our research advisors, Meredith, Jules, and I locked in a $100,000 corporate sponsor for our next big event in Los Angeles. It was a great day, but Project A.L.S. needed to wrap up early, at about four o'clock. Lorna, Karen, and I needed to get me washed and dressed for Katie, who was coming to my bed that night with Warren Beatty. I fell in love with Warren Beatty when he fell in love with Natalie Wood in *Splendor in the Grass* on the Million-Dollar Movie. I wondered what Warren was going to say about my mask, or if he would acknowledge it at all. He would probably say something funny about it, and comforting and helpful. I was so nervous to meet him. But you had to have faith in the man. I looked forward to making a new friend.

Chapter Ten

I LOVED LORNA more than life. She was my arms and legs, but she was totally clueless when it came to my hair.

"Just do a comb-over," I said, sitting and waiting on my bed as Lorna attempted a last-minute blow-dry.

"I *am* doing it," she said. But she wasn't, folks, not even close. My dryer came with attachments, which should have made her job easier, but Lorna struggled. She cast the blow-dryer in the general direction of my skull and missed—again. She might as well have been fishing for sea bass. I couldn't move at all to help Lorna help me. It was just plain crazy. This game had been going on for an hour. I was already late for my plane.

My plane and I were taking off for a luxurious six-day vacation at the Dorado Hotel in San Juan, Puerto Rico. Meredith and Peter were coming, too. Oh, and so was Reed. I'd invited him and he'd said yes. We hadn't seen each other in a year. I heard Reed drop his bags in the living room while Lorna and I focused on getting ready. I was extremely nervous to see Reed and for him to see me with the mask. Thankfully, my breathing was decent enough so that I didn't have to wear it for most of the day. I looked forward to some real face time with Reed on the beach.

It took a village just to get me out the door. While Lorna worked the hair, Karen's perfect bun spun out like a pinwheel. She was rushing around, packing a hundred suitcases filled with the bi-pap and its backup, my volume ventilator (which gave me little puffs of forced air when I didn't quite need the sustained support of the bi-pap), fifty feet of plastic tubing, extra wheelchair parts, a dozen bean-filled pillows, and my vacation wardrobe. Nothing was harder than packing clothes for Puerto Rico. My fashion choices had become limited to what I call pull-ups—basically, pants without form, zippers, or buttons. Pull-ups were modified sweatpants and, although I was never a sweatpants kind of girl, I'd set out to find the chicest pull-ups out there. Karen stacked them and packed them. I'd also bought a couple of pastel cotton tops to match, just in case a certain someone in San Juan wanted to go under my shirt for any reason.

As the precious moments to takeoff ticked away, I barked orders from the bed. I was the Scarlett O'Hara of ALS. I liked things just so. "Don't forget the ambu-bag," I reminded Karen. The ambu-bag was what Julianna Margulies had in mind when she ran down the hall shouting "Bag her!" on *ER*. It was a collapsible plastic bottle that people could use to force air into my lungs in case of an emergency—an electrical outage, for example. I had two ambu-bags, one pink and one purple.

"Ambu-bags, packed and ready—*yesterday,*" said Karen, glaring at me. She was so prideful.

"Extra mask for the bi-pap?" I asked, ticking off must-haves.

"Extra mask, check-*m,*" said Karen.

"I think you forgot the Annick Goutal," I said. I wanted to bring along my favorite moisturizer, Annick Goutal. I loved the way it smelled. I thought that Reed might like it, too.

"Annick Goutal packed *yesterday,*" said Karen. "Correction—*last week-m.*"

"Maybe *you* want to dry my hair then?" I asked Karen. I was intrigued by the lilt in Karen's speech. Being from Trinidad and Tobago she added sweet little *m* garnishes to words sometimes. Late at night, as Karen and I talked about life, death-*m,* and my chances of marrying Jon Stewart, I found her lilt comforting, like a song. At moments like these, with my plane revving up for my first vacation in six years, I found the lilt completely irritating.

"If the lady thinks her hair is important above all else-*m,* I shall drop what I'm doing and fix the lady's hair," said Karen. When it came to witty banter, the Algonquin Round Table had nothing on Karen and me. We tossed it around the infield pretty good. But repartee was a luxury that neither of us could afford at the moment. I had to get to Teterboro Airport in New Jersey or miss my flight to

Puerto Rico. Meredith and Peter called. They'd been waiting for us at the airport since breakfast.

"I don't know what you're worried about," said Valerie, who had stopped by my bed with coffee and a blueberry muffin to say bon voyage. Valerie had built great momentum with our team of scientists pursuing gene therapy. An announcement was due any day. To Valerie, a vacation at the beach meant nothing compared to the possibility she'd receive news of further progress in the lab.

"It's a private plane," Valerie reminded me, giving me sips of hot coffee from Jessie's, my new favorite deli. "*They* wait for *you*." Silly me, forgetting. That plane wasn't leaving without me. It wasn't *moving* until I dried my hair. That plane was *my* plane, a shiny Gulfstream IV, the ultimate in luxury.

My existence had become a surreal mix of loss, pain, accomplishment, and, now, ultimate luxury. As Project A.L.S. caught on as a movement, generous people came out of the woodwork to give my sisters and me support and advice, and to pave my working days with comfort. Thanks to Katie Couric, and to pieces in *The New York Times, People, Science, The New York Observer, Nature, InStyle, Forbes,* and *The Wall Street Journal* that chronicled the strides we were making in research and in fundraising, Project A.L.S. was receiving national attention. As a result, scientists and philanthropists approached us with ideas. My sisters and I were busier than we had ever been in our lives. And, frankly, I became a bit of a celebrity. My hard work was paying off. I was living the life that I dreamed of as a girl: other people packing my bags, a handsome man waiting for me in the living room, private planes and limousines. No autographs, please.

Believe me, I was perfectly happy traveling commercial, that is, until about a year and a half into ALS, when Simon and I took a horrifying Continental Airlines flight from New York to Los Angeles for a Project A.L.S. fund-raiser. We had the worst time. It was devastating, really, seeing service-oriented professionals treat people in wheelchairs like animals. The flight crew told Simon and me that the FAA didn't allow standard wheelchairs on airplanes. Fair enough, but in order to board, they said, Simon had to transfer me to a standard issue . . . it wasn't a chair, really, but a rickety toy wagon. It was fine for a doll. Simon and I had a feeling it would break any second. As soon as we loaded in, he was hauling me down the aisle like a crazed shopper. I felt like the groceries. When the FAA banned standard wheelchairs from commercial flights, you'd think that maybe it would have created a comfortable, humane alternative. The flight staff was rude to Simon and me for the entire flight. These people seemed so miserable in their jobs. We got a lot of those annoyed "special needs" glares from flight attendants whispering in the galley. After we landed, the pilot tried to squeeze by me in the aisle. But Simon and I were having trouble getting me back on the toy wagon.

"What's the holdup here?" the pilot demanded of a flight attendant. He didn't even have the courtesy to address me directly. The flight attendant rolled her eyes, while Simon tried desperately to balance me.

"I can't wait for *this*," the pilot said, meaning me. Maybe he was late for a meeting with the FAA. Finally, he kicked my wagon and stepped right over me. Simon and I were shaken to our core by the experience. When Meredith and Valerie saw our faces after landing at LAX, they thought that something terrible had happened. It took me a few hours to stop shaking. Simon and I needed a vacation just from the flight.

The next time I had to be in Los Angeles for work, I decided to phone in from my bed. The prospect of flying again was too humiliating. Then Chris and Dana Reeve offered me a ride to Los Angeles in a private plane. Chris flew all the time for work. When Dana called to offer me a lift, I started to cry. Their gesture was so incredibly generous. If not for the Reeves, I would never have seen L.A. again. Through Chris and Dana, I met my future travel mates, Bobby, Robert, Andreas, and Cynthia, three strong, handsome firefighters and an excellent nurse, who specialized in helping Chris travel the world. Thanks to the Reeves, I built my very own entourage.

I never flew commercial again. Project A.L.S. board member Brad Grey, who had lost his grandfather and mentor Sam Levin to ALS, made sure I flew safely from then on. Brad and Richard Santulli, the charitable chairman of NetJets, purveyor of the finest private aircraft in the world, donated Gulfstream jets to Project A.L.S. when I needed to go somewhere. Mr. Santulli, a man I'd never met, an angel, gave me my wings. From then on, I flew high and proud and safely.

Private airplanes were only part of my fun. There were diamonds, huge rocks that the jeweler Harry Winston gave me on loan to wear to Project A.L.S. benefits. The earrings came with their own armed guard. I did the red carpet in my Harry Winstons. Simon pushed me alongside my better-known friends Ben Stiller, Brooke Shields, Helen Hunt, Scott Wolf, and Richard Kind. We made our way down red carpets together to speak with journalists wanting to know more about Project A.L.S.

Once our whirlwind tour started, it didn't end. Project A.L.S. was named *Vanity Fair* magazine's "it" charity. I sat for a photo session with the renowned photographer Brigitte Lacombe. Charlie Rose interviewed two of our scientists, Valerie, and me on his TV show. I chatted with George Clooney and Sheryl Crow in green rooms. *Glamour* magazine awarded me Woman of the Year. Restaurateur and chef Bobby Flay came by to cook dinner for me and twelve of my best friends. When Lorna wasn't available, the John Barrett Salon of Bergdorf Goodman provided me with the full range of complimentary beauty services bedside: Nicole cut and blow-dried my hair. Rosa gave me manicures. Mercedes did eyebrows and makeup. Thomas did my color, navigating obstacles posed by the bulky bi-pap and the fact that my neck was so weak it couldn't support my head. Thomas was a magician, gentle, sweet, and talented. The John

Barrett team made sure that my hair remained my best asset and that I always looked my best. My bed became a celebrity landmark. Tired and weary from pacing the Hollywood Walk of Fame, celebrities came to my bed just to say hello.

My sisters were hot tamales, as well. Valerie and Meredith appeared in public and on TV. Clothing designers offered to dress them. My sisters and I appeared on *Entertainment Tonight* and *Access Hollywood* in Calvin Klein and Salvatore Ferragamo. When in L.A., Ricky Benjamin, driver to the stars and the owner of a sleek, wheelchair-friendly van, took me and mine wherever we wanted to go—into the Hollywood Hills, out to a beach-side restaurant in Santa Monica, the Bel-Air Hotel, please. It was dizzying. The champagne wishes and caviar dreams that I had always had for my sisters and me were finally coming true. And I was dying.

If you want a job done right, call a firefighter. Bobby and Robert carried me onto the plane at Teterboro as if it were nothing. Reed put me on his lap. I asked him to help me on with my new Chanel sunglasses, a present from Meredith for the trip. Then he held me tight as we sank down into our plush leather bucket seat for takeoff. Reed's arms around me, his legs wrapped around mine steadying me for flight—well, it definitely beat a seat belt. We fit together so well. Taxiing down the runway I thought, *How can this guy not be in love with me?* I looked at Meredith and Peter. They were so great-looking, so at home on the Gulfstream IV, and so in love with each other. The Hulberts always appeared windswept—like they were coming *back* from a vacation. I felt grateful that my sisters and I were tasting luxury, maybe not under optimal circumstances, but together in our lifetimes. I smiled at Meredith. She smiled at me. After the pilot and flight attendant wished us a good flight, we cued up Frank Sinatra on the CD player. The Gulfstream engine roared like a jungle cat, and we were number one for takeoff. As Frankie sang us up, up, up into the bluest sky, I thought that it all happens so fast, ultimately. The day starts and you can't imagine how you'll get through it—then you're through it.

Red rose petals were there at my feet when we landed. My mother's friend Linda Singer, a travel agent, made sure that my room at the Dorado was appointed with fragrant red petals, bottles of wine, and a view of the water. As the first order of business, everyone—Reed, Peter, Meredith, Lorna, Cynthia, Robert, and Bobby—carried me on a lounge chair, just like Cleopatra, down to the water. On our way to the water we said hi to the hotel staff, who were already setting up for our private beach barbecue that night. They told us to expect a singular evening, a mariachi band at sunset and plenty of horses, my favorite creatures. Everyone set me down at the edge of the sand. Then Reed transferred me into the water. He carried me out until the water was up to our shoulders. Warm waves broke around us. Reed held me deep in the ocean all afternoon. It was the most romantic moment of my life.

In the water with Reed I could move again. There wasn't gravity where we were. I was free. I looked toward the shore. My entourage stood watching us. Reed swung me around. I looked out at the ocean. It was endless. My life stretched both ways, I realized, to the shore, where I was going to have a barbecue, and toward the other end of the ocean, where my future was. Reed and I held each other in the water between the shore and infinity. There wasn't much for us to say. We just looked at each other. Then it was time to move on.

Later, before dinner, Reed tried to get the two of us into a hammock. That wasn't happening. As he lowered us down, we flipped over and I hit the deck. I felt totally humiliated. I mean, I was a grown woman lying there, unable to move at all. It was very Humpty Dumpty. My ALS had progressed to the point where even Reed didn't know if he could get me up from the ground. He shouted for Lorna. Then he stepped back to assess the situation.

"Jen," he asked, "is there anything you can do about the diet?"

"Reed," I said, "you have just crossed a line that I don't think you'll come back from."

Just then we caught sight of Lorna strolling over with the ambu-bag. She sure was taking her sweet time. I don't know what had gotten into Lorna, the sea air, sheer exhaustion from a morning of blow-drying, maybe, but there she was with the ambu-bag tucked into her arm like a purse, soaking up the sights, conversing with the birds. When Reed and I saw Lorna coming down the lane, we looked at each other and we started to laugh, tears mixed with sweat. Then we were hysterical, laughing and inconsolable. Lorna walked along just smelling the flowers while Reed and I laughed all night.

Most people get skeleton-thin from ALS. Naturally, I was the first person in the two-hundred-year history of the disease to gain weight. My neurologist, Dr. Rowland, who had seen more cases of ALS than any living person, claimed he'd never witnessed anything like it.

"Can you go on a diet?" Dr. Rowland asked as he sat on my bed during a house call.

"You want me to go on a diet?" The indignities, the mortification, the humiliation never stopped. "I have a better idea, Bud. Why don't you give me some medicine to help me breathe?"

"Let's see what you and your sisters come up with," he said. "I have my fingers crossed." Dr. Rowland—my own doctor—was relying on Project A.L.S. to come up with medicine for ALS. How crazy was that? I have to admit, it was gratifying as well. Bud Rowland was truly impressed with the research progress that Project A.L.S. was making. As for the weight gain, the truth is, I wasn't eating that much.

"Are you sure, Jenifer?" asked Meredith, who understood my tendency to pack it away in private.

"I swear," I swore. It's not like I could just roll into the kitchen and grab a box of cookies. If anything, ALS brought my stormy love affair with food to an end. Food and I fell in love when I was a baby girl. Our house could have been burning down. Give me a Twinkie, I was happy. I wasn't inhibited around food. If I wanted something, I ate it. I was free. When Kaka came to New York for the first time to visit us as grown-up girls, I prepared her a surprise platter of cut-up Twinkies and attractive wedges of Hostess cupcakes. I couldn't think of a better way to welcome my baby-sitter from Rock Island. Food warmed and comforted me. It smelled good, looked good; it satisfied every time.

Then when I hit thirteen, my relationship with food turned illicit. It became my secret lover. I snuck it. I felt embarrassed for wanting it. As I grew, so to speak, I felt further and further from my body ideal, also known as the Harrison High School cheerleaders. Realistically, I probably had ten or fifteen pounds to lose, but the girl I saw in the mirror was way bigger. I dieted and dieted. I failed and failed. I wasn't alone. Every girl I knew wanted to change her shape, even the Harrison High School cheerleaders. Every girl dieted. Every girl failed. We girls couldn't win for losing. Dieting seemed rigged to me, like pro wrestling. Still, I couldn't take myself out of the game. As a single healthy woman in New York, I spent many nights at home alone feeling "not quite right" when I could have been out there. I tried taking Valerie's advice and accepting my body for what it was. But sustained self-criticism, which girls seem to learn as willingly as boys learn the fundamentals of baseball, came more naturally.

Several years into ALS, I wasn't even eating real meals anymore. The truth is, I could barely swallow. When ALS told my muscles to let go, they did as they were told, systematically, every last one of them, including those I used to chew and swallow food. My favorite things to eat—turkey on a roll, roasted chicken, Caesar salad—were too dangerous for me to try, so I said goodbye to them. For the first time in my life I didn't look forward to eating—I feared it. I was afraid of choking. Lorna, Karen, and Juliet cut up my food and fed me like a baby. Eventually they ran everything through a blender three times. Meredith and Valerie brought over their own liquid creations for me to try—cream of cream of cream of broccoli soup, gravy with a dollop of mashed potatoes. Nothing went down easy. My days of taking food by mouth were numbered. Yet, incredibly, I gained weight.

I called myself Puff Jenny—P. Jiddy to the inner circle. As I lost muscles, I lost muscle tone. As I lost muscle tone, I began to look like another person. Unfortunately, that person wasn't especially slender. She was puffy, really puffy. I was never a small girl, but ALS cut me down and blew up my ass. It was a shame. I'd peaked physically before I got sick. I was thirty-five at the time, a little late in the game maybe, but I was coming to a new understanding of my body. Thanks to working out and eating right, I'd never felt more beautiful. ALS was my tough luck: I wasn't eating and I gained weight . . . I was wearing the Queen's diamonds on my ears, but I could hardly hold my head up to support them . . . I was running a multimillion-dollar company devoted to wiping out a disease that had already destroyed my body, piece by piece. My plate was full and I couldn't eat.

Puerto Rico proved that although I wasn't at my best physically, I could still feel beautiful. Reed had something to do with that, I think. But beauty, as in looking my best, had always been of the utmost importance. Best foot forward—best smile, best hair, and best face, no matter what. I worked to present my best self to the world, always with a little lipstick. I discovered my own look and went full tilt in that direction. As a girl, I accepted that there were movie stars whom I didn't and could never look like. There were certain women, however—Cher, Barbra Streisand—whose looks seemed totally achievable. I liked Cher because I looked like her. I really loved Barbra Streisand. In every photo, film, or song, she seemed to be saying: *Just because I have a big nose, don't tell me I can't have everything I want.* I liked her subtext. Just because I wasn't Lana Turner didn't mean I should jump off a cliff. So I worked it. I started by copying Cher, and I kind of jumped off from there. I grew up knowing that *my style* was terrific and beautiful and the only one that counted. I knew it on an intellectual level, anyway. In reality, doing the day was incredibly challenging, no matter what I wore. Doing the day was my life's work. It was hard work.

When I got ALS, I craved beauty. I filled up my senses with it. More things were beautiful to me. My palette expanded—along with my figure—when I got sick. To me, the sight of working legs was beautiful. A cheeseburger deluxe was beautiful. Meredith brushing Jane's hair into a ponytail was beautiful. I still admired the undeniable beauty of, say, a Michelle Pfeiffer. It's just that my scope was so much bigger now. My capacity to take it all in—Martha's eyes, Willis's hands, Valerie's face when she promised that everything was going to be okay—was limitless. Was I *beautiful* rolling down the red carpet in a wheelchair all puffy with no husband or children, and no foreseeable future? I guess so. I guess I was beautiful, in a way. I had learned to take it all in. That's not to say I'd ruled out plastic surgery. As God is my witness, I vowed that if I ever got better I'd haul it in for a total body lift. Just pull the whole thing up and over and get out the scissors. Until then and after that I would cherish every beautiful moment: *Just because I have a big nose and a World War II mask in this wheelchair, don't tell me I can't have everything I want.*

Did Reed dig my look in Puerto Rico? Was he attracted to me for ten seconds? I'm gonna go out on a limb and say yes, but I'll never know for sure. Nothing happened between us at the beach in San Juan, except for everything. We didn't sleep. We talked all day and night for six days. Reed rubbed my shoulders. He lay down next to me on the bed. He put his forehead against mine and we laughed. The sound of the checkout notice sliding under the door of my hotel room at four in the morning signaled the end.

The moment my Gulfstream IV hit the New Jersey runway, Reed bolted for L.A. It was like the worst part of *Cinderella*. We hit the ground and my private plane turned into a filthy wheelchair van . . . my entourage turned into nurses and firefighters who had to get home to their own families . . . Meredith and Peter turned into parents talking reassuringly into their cell phones to their kids, who'd missed them terribly . . . and Reed, my prince, turned into a guy who couldn't wait to get home to walk his dog. I guess that made me Cinderella, wheelchair strapped in, trying to keep her balance during a bumpy van ride home to Manhattan.

We'd all had a beautiful time in Puerto Rico, a great vacation. As I was loaded out of the van and onto my bed on Twelfth Street, I was filled with sensations of Puerto Rico: Reed and me in the hammock; him helping me touch a white horse that walked up to us on the beach; Lorna strolling along with the ambu-bag; being in the water with Reed, Meredith and Peter watching us from the shore. Then the sensations went away. By the time Karen and I settled in for my welcome-home foot massage, I couldn't feel Puerto Rico anymore. It was weird how fast moments turned into memories.

No life of beauty and glamour is complete without a movie being made about it. After we returned from Puerto Rico, I heard that the documentary filmmaker and HBO honcho Sheila Nevins was interested in coming to the bed. I knew Sheila to be a big deal. She had a trunkful of Academy Awards. She was one of the first women to make it big as an entertainment executive. Sheila Nevins was known for speaking her mind.

Sheila came to my bed with Sara Bernstein, her colleague at HBO. She told Valerie, Meredith, and me that she'd heard a lot about Project A.L.S. *She's me,* I thought as Sheila walked to the bed, this woman who was living the life I wanted. She was a great businesswoman, funny, self-deprecating, creative, so powerful. We sat with Sheila and Sara for a while, not really knowing why they'd come. After spending an hour together, Sheila said she wanted to do a movie about us, a documentary for HBO. She asked if she and her crew could come to my apartment in two weeks and film my sisters and me right on the bed. In three months, Sheila and HBO put the finishing touches on *Three Sisters: Searching for a Cure,* a forty-minute film that captured the essence of Project A.L.S. Brad Grey had just formed Plan B Films, which produced *Three Sisters.*

At last, my big-screen debut. It wasn't glamorous. There I am in the movie with my bi-pap cranking and my Hannibal Lecter mask. I look pretty ravaged up there. "Oh, well," I said to Willis, as we watched a rough, rough cut.

"You're the prettiest woman on earth, Jen," he said.

My movie debut felt like my swan song. Late at night, when my sisters went home, I began feeling a restlessness that was hard to describe. For six years of ALS, I could always lean on whatever function I had left. When my legs became paralyzed, I leaned on my arms. When my neck was paralyzed, I leaned on my trunk. I loved my lips and mouth. Now they were going. I was having trouble forming words. Now I had nothing left to lean on, except for Valerie and Meredith, the loves of my life.

Valerie reported to me deep into the night by e-mail about gene therapy, her work with scientists and the NIH and the FDA, and now our first move to human trial. We were getting closer to a shot for me, she promised. She urged me to hang in there. All I could think was that the upper right side of my lip was going.

Meredith called me one morning after taking the kids to school.

"No one understands what I'm saying anymore," I told her.

"You sound clear as a bell to me," she said.

"Katie, Martha, Caroline—I say something and every-one says *What? What did you say?*" I said.

"Wait a second. I think I just heard the doorbell," said Meredith. I knew there was no doorbell ringing.

"You don't understand what I'm saying, do you, Merry?" I said. More and more, when we spoke on the phone, Valerie and Meredith suddenly had to get doorbells ringing or pots burning on the stove or save children from falling on knives. My sisters created these smoke screens because they couldn't quite bring themselves to tell me the truth—that more and more they didn't understand what I was saying. My lips and mouth were getting weaker. I couldn't wrap them around my words. Not being able to sit on the bed talking with Valerie and Meredith—that was my life. It had always been my life. ALS was taking my speech, my last remaining treasure. ALS had shaken me down to my last penny. I tried to be strong.

Why me? You've asked that question, I'm sure. I have. My sisters have. Why us? Why did a fatal disease with no medicine break up our miraculous love and cut it short? I don't know. All I know is that everyone has a *why me.* Look at Christie Brinkley. You wouldn't think she has a *why me,* but I bet she does. Look at your parents and friends. Look at your children. Look in the mirror. Everyone faces a challenge—or not, as they so choose. Everyone has a *why me.* I got a pretty bad one. But the key for me and my sisters had always been looking at our *why me* straight on and getting to work, getting to love, in the time we had left.

"I still think we're gonna get out of this," said Meredith, as we sat on the bed, the bi-pap cycling air in and out, sounding like waves in a mechanical ocean. This was our millionth "I still think we're gonna get out of this" pep talk. Meredith always kicked it off, followed by Valerie's saying yes, we'd definitely get out of it, followed by my saying I hoped we'd get out of it. That was the script, but this millionth time, everyone forgot their lines.

"I do," said Meredith. "I think we'll get out of it, but we really have to move it along."

"Hmmm," I said.

"We've gotta get out of this," said Valerie.

"I think there's still a chance," said Meredith.

"You know," I said, "even if we don't get out of this, we're still getting out of it." I knew I was right. My sisters knew I was right. Maybe science wasn't going to catch up with me. Maybe it was, but it probably wasn't. All I knew was that Project A.L.S. was going to fight and push and work and love until ALS was gone. This disease was going down.

"Bring it on," I said, as Lorna brought me my last cup of coffee on earth on the bed. A few months after I got back from Puerto Rico, I officially declared my swallowing shot. Lorna tipped the cup to my mouth, and the coffee from Jessie's Deli went down. The hot coffee warmed me inside out. Life was just so beautiful.

Chapter Eleven

WHEN I WAS in high school, August was about inhaling, going to the beach with Meredith, and exhaling. That was the rhythm of our days. Every day in August, Meredith and I drove to Sherwood Island in Connecticut to work on our tans between the peak hours of noon and two. Windows down, our hair blew wild. I remember the sun on my face. I remember the sun on Meredith's face as she drove. Meredith always drove. She said I was a horrible driver. Fine with me—I wanted my own chauffeur someday anyway; so did she, for that matter. There was no doubt about it. One day we were going to live in huge houses side by side with our own chauffeurs. Driving with Meredith, deep breaths, the reassurance of the Connecticut tides—it was all very August.

Then August changed. After six and a half years of being sick, I watched the summer grow dark from my window. August became the dark, stormy heath of reckoning where Shakespeare's characters ranted and raved about betrayal and lost children. At first the heath was pretty quiet, as in "all's quiet on the western heath." Then the wind kicked up. From my bed I watched the summer wind blow with a vengeance. Was I the only one to notice? The wind had a personality all of a sudden. It wanted me dead.

Then King Lear, make that Valerie, marched in.

"I wanna kill someone. I just wanna wipe the idiotic looks off people's faces." Spoken like the director of scientific research for Project A.L.S. Valerie paced back and forth in front of the bed.

"Lorna," I said.

"Coming," said Lorna, who came quicker from the living room these days. Lorna was on high alert in August.

"We need to go out and down with the mask," I said. Lorna pulled the mask away from my face and shifted it downward. Still not right.

"Out and down, Lorna," I repeated. Lorna, a home health aide who had become the most skilled ALS caregiver on the face of the planet, tried and failed again to reposition the mask on my face. I couldn't get a decent breath in August. Lorna and I spent hours at a time just trying to get the mask to sit properly. Valerie paced, fuming at the world, Lorna, and me.

"I'm the one you want to kill," I said to Valerie as Lorna tightened the Velcro straps that held the mask in place. "I'm the one who ruined your life."

"Why do you have to be so selfish?" Valerie said.

"Why does everything have to revolve around you? I have my own life, Jenifer. I have my own problems that have nothing whatsoever to do with you."

"That's why I think you should go home and be with your children," I said. The sicker I got, the harder Valerie and Meredith worked. They worked in the living room, on the bed. They never went home.

"We're this close to medicine and you want me to go home?" she said. Valerie raged in August. It was too bad. Things couldn't have been more promising from the research side. For one thing, it was official: Dr. Gage's gene therapy helped ALS mice to live over one-third longer than untreated ALS mice. These stunning findings were about to be published in the prestigious journal *Science* and announced all over the news. It was the best therapeutic result seen in the history of the disease. According to Valerie's calculations, the gene therapy human trial would begin in a little over a year. She demonstrated where I'd be getting my shots. They were going to inject my neck and my legs and my arms and my chest.

"They better hurry up," I said.

"Just don't you worry," said Valerie, as if she knew something I didn't. I was so proud of her. Valerie had put the scientists together. She had mothered them, exacting best efforts from them. Gene therapy was only the beginning. Stem cells continued to show great therapeutic promise. Project A.L.S. researchers were also zeroing in on "disease pathways," or why ALS occurred in the first place. On account of Project A.L.S., the research community was working together as a family—as the family that would beat ALS. If August was dark and disturbing from my window, the landscape of ALS had never appeared sunnier.

Valerie fell at my feet and cried. She said she'd been doing a lot of that lately, feeling angry, then sad. She raged, then mourned, and she didn't know why. I knew why.

Meredith came in. Let's call her Viola, Lady Macbeth, and Juliet—all of the women of Shakespeare plus the sonnets—wrapped up into one majestic twenty-first-century mama. For six years, Meredith had searched the world for meaning and money for research. She built Project A.L.S. from "an Ikea desk and two milk crates"—as the actor Richard Kind had once said about us—into a $20 million company. She had drafted thousands of Americans into the unpopular war against brain disease. I was so proud of her. Meredith, too, was in a foul mood.

"Is this *it* for you and work?" she asked me, glaring. "Just tell me because I need to know. We have three events coming up. If I *can't* count on you I need to know *now.*"

"Suction, Lorna," I said. In August Lorna stood by my bed like a soldier. My swallowing muscles had grown dangerously weak. We used a machine to suction my so-called secretions, or saliva, because swallowing—just regular everyday swallowing—made me choke. Lorna inserted the plastic suction tube into my mouth.

"Just tell me who to call, Merry," I said over the whirring of the machine, "and I'll call."

"That's what you said last week," said Meredith. I wanted to keep working from the bed but, truth be told, I usually didn't have the energy. In all my forty years, I'd never let anyone down on the job, but here we were. Who knew that an honest day's work was one of life's great luxuries? Meredith was fit to be tied in August. She wasn't sleeping and she didn't know why. I knew why.

I got pneumonia. Pneumonia is to ALS what fire is to the Scarecrow. It came on in an instant, and because I couldn't move, breathe, cough, or clear my throat or lungs, the infection settled in my lungs and spread fast. My lungs filled with fluid. It's funny saying this, but besides the ALS I was actually a pretty healthy person. I couldn't remember the last time I had had a fever. But I was burning hot. Nadine, an excellent registered nurse, or RN, was on duty that day. I couldn't afford to be without an RN anymore. My situation called for the heavy artillery, major RNs like Juliet Hercules, Nadine Donohue, Maureen Carlo, veterans of the wars. These chicks didn't mess around. Along with Karen and Lorna, they threw me onto my side, sat me up, pounded my chest and back, gave me Heimlich maneuvers. They dripped sweat daily to keep my systems cleared. They knew my body better than a husband. In rare moments of respite they heard my confessions. I told them how I feared for Valerie's and Meredith's future and for the future of their children, my children, without me. I confided my deepest emotions to these women I barely knew. I obsessed with thoughts of Valerie and Meredith in a world without me. *Will they be okay without me? Will they be okay?* My nurses listened. They told me I wasn't going anywhere and that I didn't have to worry about such things. In wartime my nurses and I spent each second fighting together for the next.

When my temperature hit 102 degrees, Nadine called 911. St. Vincent's Hospital was located conveniently right across the street. Nadine, Valerie, and the paramedics put me on a stretcher and ran me and my bi-pap right over to the St. Vincent's emergency room, where an X-ray of my chest revealed a left lung black with fluid. I choked and burned with fever. Dale Ryan, a nurse in the ER, made it right. Dale set me up. She got an IV line in me—no small task, because I had extremely hard-to-find veins—and kept me hydrated and nourished. Nurse Ryan had pounded a few chests in her time. She talked to me in a kind voice and stroked my hair. Dr. Linda Kirshenbaum—or Dr. K., as my sisters and I called her—an expert in emergency medicine, took me up to the critical care unit. Dale and Dr. K. became instant family. I stayed in the CCU at St. Vincent's for almost a week until I responded to antibiotics and stabilized. I was the youngest person there. Valerie and Meredith lived in the waiting area of the CCU for that week. They didn't leave my side.

Cameras were rolling in earnest on the latest movie in my head, *The Beds of August,* a new comedy-drama about a woman so sick she goes from bed to bed to bed, all over the city. That very night, only a few hours home from the hospital, I "threw a plug," a Shakespearean term that my nurse Maureen used to describe the sudden inability to clear mucus. Mucus obstructed my airway while I was watching TV, and I lost consciousness immediately. Karen called 911.

This time I was totally out of it. The paramedics couldn't find a pulse on me. They put me on the floor and worked to bring me back. I don't remember much—the sense of gentle men's voices and Karen calling Valerie on my phone, telling her to hurry over. Later, Valerie told me it had looked like a nativity scene when she got there. It was four in the morning. My room was lit by a lamp, she said. Paramedics worked around me on the floor quietly, lovingly, expertly. Karen stood over them with her hands clasped. Valerie knelt at my feet.

"Got a pulse," said one of the paramedics after a while.

"I love you, Jenifer," said Valerie. "I love you." I loved her so much. I heard Valerie, but I couldn't reach her. I didn't see a white light or a tunnel. All I felt was a wanting to get back to my sister, a reaching, the same reaching I'd always felt when I was near her and Meredith. I reached as I always had—to get back, start over, do better.

"You can't leave anyway," Valerie said. "Do you hear me? You're gonna be on Katie in an hour." At Valerie's mention of the *Today* show, on which the results of our gene therapy work were to be announced that very morning, I opened one eye. I was back. In the end death was no match for my chance to appear on national television.

"Jenifer," Valerie said, holding me.

"I'm here," I said, opening my eyes. And back we went to the ER at St. Vincent's. My bed there was still warm. Dr. K. was none too pleased to see me again. She felt that at this rate I was asking for big trouble. She wanted to perform a tracheotomy, immediately. She wanted one of her colleagues to cut a hole in my neck and attach a ventilator to the hole. Arguably, having "the trach," as they call it in ALS circles, would make my breathing and the act of suctioning a little easier. But after having given the matter much thought over the years, I had already decided against the trach. As it was, I had adapted so much in so many ways to being sick. Living with a trach and all that that meant—the constant need for suction, a nurse by my side every second of every day, probable loss of my already waning ability to speak and eat—wasn't for me. Dr. K. felt we needed to move on it right away.

Valerie called her team at Johns Hopkins. The Hopkins doctors, led by Dr. Jeff Rothstein, had evolved into the leading clinical team in the country. They were amazing that day. Dr. Charlie Weiner, associate director of medicine at Hopkins, who had had extensive experience helping ALS patients to breathe, took the next Amtrak north to New York to assess me. I had never even met Charlie, and there he was by my side. Charlie told Dr. K. he thought that I could go for years more on the bi-pap. In fact, he said, he'd never seen a patient use a bi-pap for so long and look so good.

I was feeling cocky. I had narrowly escaped the trach. Still, because I had aspirated or choked the night before, Charlie and Dr. K. agreed that I needed to have a feeding tube surgically inserted into my stomach as soon as possible. At this point, food going down the wrong way would mean instant death. They shipped me uptown to Columbia Presbyterian for the procedure.

The most uncomfortable bed of August was the one at Columbia Presbyterian, where I had my feeding tube inserted. The staff was slightly off during my stay—a lot of people entering without knocking.

"You know ALS doesn't affect the hearing," I said to one resident who recited my vital signs to me very s-l-o-w-l-y and very LOUDLY. "I understand what you're saying," I reiterated. I wanted him to know that ALS didn't affect my cognition, either. I also wanted to give Columbia the benefit of the doubt. I loved Columbia. Project A.L.S. had directed some nice cash to research at the university; my neurologist, Dr. Rowland, was a Columbia man; three of the five treasured research advisors to Project A.L.S. resided at Columbia, including Gerry Fischbach, an elegant researcher, advocate, and now dean of the Columbia Medical School. It was August, after all—maybe the neurology unit's A Team was on vacation.

One young neurologist said he needed to take a blood gas—a painful blood test that measures the level of oxygen in the blood—right away. Earlier that afternoon I had asked his supervisor if instead of the blood gas I might get a good night's rest. The supervisor thought that rest was a great idea and that I could just as well have my blood drawn the next day. Late that night the young neurologist snuck into my room, as determined to take my blood as I was powerless to move. He stuck my wrist over and over. He couldn't find my artery. My wrist was bloody and bruised the next morning.

No matter how hard you fight to maintain your dignity in the foxhole, you can expect moments of humiliation and disappointment. There's no avoiding them. These moments are built in to the life-and-death experience. I didn't know if that young neurologist meant to one-up me or his boss—and I didn't care. I was sure that the millions of people sick and dying from untreatable brain diseases in fine hospitals all over the country didn't care, either. Putting up with the humiliations, these unfortunate moments made of man's inhumanity to man, would be so much easier for us to bear—if we just had some medicine.

When you're in the foxhole you have to thank the stars for people like Daniel Brodie, a young doctor who I believe represents the future of medicine. Dr. Brodie, a pulmonology fellow, came to my bed at Columbia not knowing me but curious to meet me. Daniel was so kind. We talked for hours about breathing and my chances for survival. Amazingly, I still had the strength to appreciate a good-looking doctor. Life without romance isn't worth pursuing. I looked at Daniel Brodie knowing that his life would be richly romantic, as mine had been. He had a light in his eyes. He had a passion for work that I recognized. My romantic imagination was still a comfort to me, even that August in the foxhole. I had always worked to keep romance alive in some form. When I didn't have true love in my life, I got by with fantasies, memories, and crushes. They were all part of my workout until the real thing came along. Visits from Daniel Brodie kept me sharp in August. He entered my romantic imagination and, as a result, I felt prepared. I was ready for anything.

My bed had served as a temple, a stage, a place where I learned to see the world. The Beds of August—whether in the ER at St. Vincent's, in the CCU, on the neurology floor at Columbia Presbyterian, in ambulances, or at home—were foxholes. In August I hunkered down in my bed and held on as the bombs flew above me. There was no margin of error in the foxhole—one wrong move and I was a goner. Luckily, the wisdom of the foxhole, my most basic survival instincts, kicked in. They had always been there in reserve. I believed that they lived in everyone. *Live now,* I said to myself, *now and now and now.*

I talked myself through one second at a time in August and praised myself for every effort: A nurse came toward me with an ambu-bag when my bi-pap went out. *You can do this,* I thought, and I did. I put all of my energy into working with the nurse and the ambu-bag until the bi-pap was up and running again. Willis was excited for our date to watch a Johnny Depp movie on the bed, but I didn't want him to see me struggling. I wanted to cancel our plans for the sleepover. *I must do this,* I thought, and Willis and I lay next to each other watching movies all night. My nurse Maureen came toward me with a huge plastic syringe to give me my first feeding through the new plastic tube in my stomach. *This I can't do,* I thought. *I just can't do this.* I took a beat, a private moment. Was there an upside to my taking baby formula through my stomach? *Maybe these cans of crap will make me strong again.* "All right, bring on the dog food," I said, and Maureen injected a putrid, enriched formula into my brand-new stomach tube. I felt a cold sensation in my stomach. I never ate another meal. Rather I had "feedings" four times a day. I was like an animal at the zoo. My whole life I'd counted on food for everything from genuine pleasure to avoidance to celebrating with friends. Food gave me a major something to do. When my breathing went, I leaned on my ability to swallow food and drinks. When my ability to swallow went . . . I saw the sign up ahead: Beginning of the End.

When do you wave the white flag? As sick as I was, I held on to a thread of the belief that I might get better. I think that that's just the way of the human heart. The heart's desire is to be repaired. The heart beats in the name of repair from birth until the end. I longed to benefit from the breadth of knowledge, the resources and technology, the great promise and wealth of the age I lived in, of this new century. Was I a fool to believe that all good things might converge in time to save me? I wasn't a fool. I just loved my life. I wasn't a fool. I was a dreamer. I also happened to be realistic. I knew that I might die soon.

The first order of business was to make sure that if death came no one would try to jump in there with me, especially Valerie and Meredith. Obsessive thoughts of death had begun to color my days and nights. I was adamant about not sharing these thoughts with my sisters, the children, Scott and Peter, Katie, Simon, Rob, my friends, or my mother. The fear of death spreads fast in the foxhole. Fear breeds panic and chaos. I decided that showing my fear was no way for me to go on—even if I was going out. I learned that I could carry my fears with dignity. I could bear more than I ever thought. That was a revelation. The people I loved had their own pain. My pain was mine. My sisters were having a hard enough time. They were so angry.

"Love is the answer," I said to Valerie during one of her homicidal rants.

"Who are you, Mahatma Gandhi?" she screamed.

"Was Mahatma the man or the woman?" I asked. I never could keep those Gandhis straight. So accomplished, that family.

"Just leave me alone," said Valerie. But I didn't want to leave her alone. She didn't want to leave me alone, either. For all of our lives, Valerie, Meredith, and I never wanted to leave one another alone. After three trips to the hospital in August, when I was finally back at home, my sisters and I had the chance to sit on the bed and assess the big picture. With a lovely feeding tube inserted safely in my stomach and no further sign of infection, Valerie and Meredith seemed to think we had actually bought some time in August. I wished they were right.

"I hope you're right," I said.

"I'm right," said Valerie.

"Merry?" Meredith was awfully quiet.

"Hmm?" she said.

"Do you think we bought ourselves some time?" I asked.

"I guess. Yeah," Meredith said. But it was clear to me from her tone and the cloud of concern that had settled over us that we didn't know how much. My sisters and I couldn't look at one another. Their anger was giving way to sadness and a sense of defeat we weren't ready to acknowledge. We sat on the bed, each of us crying and looking away.

The big blackout of 2003 hit the next afternoon. My two generators combined delivered only five hours of backup electricity for my bi-pap. So when the lights went out, I went back to St. Vincent's. It was like old home week for me over in the ER, which was jammed with people looking for a place to rest their feet during the blackout. There wasn't a bed to be had when we arrived. Then Nurse Dale Ryan appeared. She said she'd been expecting me from the moment New York lost light.

"I knew you were coming, Jen," Dale said, leaning on my old, faithful ER stretcher she'd marked with a Day-Glo Post-it: RESERVED FOR JENIFER ESTESS. Being in the hospital during the blackout wasn't great for my body. The constant back-and-forth to hospitals in August had taken a major toll.

At the end of the day at the end of August, I worried. When I settled into sleep, I worried in my dreams. I dreamed about flying. That part was good. I dreamed I was flying up strong and free in the dark. My hair blew in the wind. Then I heard the sounds of children. The sounds awoke me with a start. I woke up worrying about the children. I looked for a sign, some assurance that— with or without me—the children would live in happiness and health. I knew that nature didn't grant such assurances. Nature was harsh. Only the fittest survived, it said. The occasional baby bird or lion cub or llama fell through the cracks, got eaten or abandoned because nature dictated it. But I thought it should be different for the children. Freeing the children from a future of disease and heartbreak—we ought to do that, by whatever means necessary. What separated humans from animals was our ability to teach nature a thing or two.

I never had children of my own. That was my greatest dream unrealized. It was my one and only personal tragedy. But in a way I always felt the love that a mother feels. I knew the power of my love and of my listening to help children grow and change. I understood the power of the words *I know you can do it* to go a really long way. I knew that with a little encouragement—true parenting—the children in my life could feel empowered to go out there, teach nature a thing or two, and change the world.

My beautiful, amazing children: Jake, Willis, Jane, James, Kate. As I turned the page from August to the winter of my life, I looked for a sign that they would be all right. My children had the best parents in the world. Meredith and Peter and Scott and Valerie would keep up the good work because their love for their children was just so huge. I wanted to tell my nieces and nephews a little something, too. I wanted them to know I wasn't scared. I wanted them to know that even if I died they would be okay.

The children would always be a-okay. I knew this for a fact because I saw them being born. Jake was the first baby. Meredith and Peter conceived Jake on my bed in my apartment on Seventy-first Street. (I was out with friends that night.) Nine months later, on March 10, Meredith's water broke on my same bed. Meredith, Peter, and I took a cab to New York University Hospital early the next morning in the snow and cold. I was always a lucky third wheel when it came to the children. I was always there at the birth. I stood by Meredith while she was in heavy labor. She was working her contractions along to a tape that Valerie had made of our favorite songs from high school. The boom box blasted and Meredith pushed. I think it was Carly Simon's "Embrace Me You Child" that put her over the top. Meredith pushed one last time and Jake was born on March 11 at 1:59 A.M. Jake was a skinny thing. He looked like a wise old man. Peter stood there in his scrubs, weeping, "It's a boy. It's a boy." The whole family came to see the first baby under the warming light of his baby bed. Jake looked like a grandpa sunbathing in Miami. Fittingly, we ordered up corned beef and knishes from Sarge's Deli and partied in the waiting room for a day and a half. Being there at the birth taught me that there was nothing to be scared of either in coming into the world or leaving it.

There had been so many births. I watched Jake grow into a strapping young man. Willis was born, my Hubbell on earth. Jane came, my spitting image, a beautiful, strong girl who put others first. Kate ran in. She was a little Jodie Foster and reminded me so much of Valerie. Then there was James, an artist in the making. James had been tentative around me. At five, he had only ever known me as a sick person. He was especially scared of the bi-pap mask. I knew how he felt. As a kid, I was scared of people who looked very ill. One night James was adamant about telling me something in private. Meredith, Peter, and the others cleared the room, and James climbed onto my bed and into my lap. James had never come onto the bed before. He had never touched me. He put his face to my ear.

"Jen Jen," he whispered, "I'm not scared of the mask anymore. I'm not scared." And he held me for a moment, climbed down, and went home. James had the heart of an artist all right. He moved right through his fear. They say that people don't change. That's hogwash as far as I was concerned. James changed. My sisters and I had changed through the years. We had become more open as women, more savvy as businesspeople, a little softer around the edges. Scientists changed. They were motivated by a new urgency to figure out ALS. Just like James, I would continue making changes. I knew that if I ever got better I sure would make at least one radical change. I'd be a lot more physical. There would be a line of men around the block waiting to have liaisons with me. Watching people change, changing my own life—that was the main attraction for me.

I started to ramble—kind of like this—after August. I started thinking about things in the abstract, which was totally unlike me. I pictured worst-case scenarios; I entertained vague visions of brighter futures—exactly whose futures they were, I didn't know. Spending a lot of time in the foxhole left me a little "general" in my thinking. I engaged in mental walkabouts. They bothered me. I knew myself. I had to commit myself to a project, something concrete, or else I'd go nuts, so I planned a combined birthday party for Willis, who had turned ten, and Jane, just nine. Lorna dressed my place with streamers and balloons. We made gift bags for everyone. According to my strict instructions, Lorna bought and wrapped almost a million presents for Willis and Jane. I ordered everyone's favorite food. Everything was in place for the big blowout.

The morning of the party I woke up early. I felt the old excitement of Christmas. I couldn't wait for my family to come that night and for the children to open their presents. Everyone waited in the living room while Lorna sat me up. Then she flung open the doors. Everyone came to the bed and we had a great time. Willis really liked the fifty-seven video games I bought him. I'm sure Jane liked her American Girl dolls. I bought her the one that she wanted, a pretty pioneer. I bought the accessories that every pioneer needed, sold separately: utensils for eating hearty meals by the fire, boots for the long trek, and a bed for resting at the end of days filled with discovery. It was the complete pioneer's package. It was a great birthday party. Lorna got ready to go home.

"When will I see you again?" I asked her.

"Tuesday morning," said Lorna.

"That's so far away," I said.

"Tuesday's close, Jenifer," she said. "It's real close." My family hung out for a while, then Karen breezed in fashionably late for her night shift.

"Everyone needs to bundle up-*m,*" she said. "It's a cold night." The passage of time is different in the foxhole. Somehow, just as Valerie's and Meredith's anger gave way to sadness, August had given way to December. I didn't remember much about the months in between. The children put on their warm coats after a great party, climbed one by one onto my bed, and I kissed them good-bye. They walked into the cold night. I never saw them again.

Chapter Twelve

I DIED ON DECEMBER 16, two days after the birthday party. It was early in the morning, a little after five. I was deep asleep and dreaming my usual. I don't know what medical event occurred. I stopped breathing is all, my heart stopped beating, and I was on my way. One second I was dreaming, the next second I was traveling.

I'm on my way, as Paul Simon says. I don't know where I'm going. Maybe to heaven or straight into the hearts of the people I love or into lettuce fields or carrot patches or cut flowers. Everyone has a guess on the matter of where we go when we die. All I know is that I'm rising. That's a good sign, don't you think? As far as general directions one wants to be heading in are concerned, up is definitely my first choice. So far it's been dark the whole way. I'm moving through a deep navy blue ocean dark that isn't scary. At this point, anything seems possible. Changes in hues, colors, or the lightness—there's no way for me to predict what's going to happen. I'm sure only of the rising. There's no more pain. I am moving again. My ALS is totally gone, which makes perfect sense. ALS can survive only if it's sucking the life out of a living, breathing human being. As of this rising, it's probably entering the nerve cells of another unsuspecting sister, brother, mother, or father. ALS isn't picky—it's an equal opportunity disease. But quite frankly now, I am pure joy. I am the joy of movement. I know that sounds like an aerobics class, but it's true. I am joy rising.

People said I looked really good dead. They said I looked the way I did before I got sick. After I died, Lorna put on my lipstick of choice, "Pearl" by Mac; she brushed my hair and put me in a black turtleneck and my favorite pants. I was a babe in that box. Friends stood over me in the hospital morgue and in my viewing room at Riverside Memorial Chapel. They loved seeing me without the Hannibal Lecter mask. I had a really pretty face. I loved my body. I'd forgotten.

"Beautiful Jenifer," said Lorna, crying as she touched my face. "You're in the arms of Jesus now." Truth be told, the cradling image kind of works for me. I find the image of being rocked in someone's arms or in the branches of a tree comforting. It gives me something to look forward to. I haven't passed any robed figures or men with beards on this ocean blue highway. I haven't seen women in gowns. No obvious angels. That's not to say I won't. I'm just moving through the dark alone now. We'll see what we see.

My last night alive was pretty usual: formula through my feeding tube for dinner at eight, a couple of hours watching TV, phone calls with Valerie and Meredith, and a foot massage. Christmas was coming. The same night of the birthday party, Valerie, Meredith, and the kids had brought up a tree and decorated it outside my room. I don't know why, but I wasn't quite ready to look at the tree. That night, for the time being, I watched reflections from its lights on my wall. My home health aides Basilia and Rosanne, who were filling in for my regular nurses, helped me off to sleep somewhere between three and four in the morning. The night was typical; the day before hadn't been.

That day, Monday, was the last time I saw Meredith, my Meredith, the daylight. We sat on the bed, working. One of our board members had been planning a power breakfast to honor Project A.L.S. Meredith and I considered the scenario. We discussed the details of the annual Project A.L.S. holiday party, which always took place in the general vicinity of my bed. Then Meredith and I checked in with *General Hospital*.

Meredith stayed later than usual. She normally took a five-something train home, but Peter was coaching Jane's basketball team that night, then taking the kids out to dinner, so Meredith and I had a few hours to hang out. My baby sister looked tired on the bed, but statuesque—always statuesque, even at her worst. I looked just horrible. My energy was at an all-time low. I could feel my airways—the intricate paths through which oxygen flows, nourishing our bodies—growing smaller by the day. My infrastructure was shrinking and caving in on itself.

"Sometimes I'm scared," I said, "that we just fade to black. That it's just lights out at the end."

"I don't think so," said Meredith.

"What do you think?" I asked.

"I don't know, but I don't think we fade to black. I mean *after all this*?"

"What are you gonna have for dinner?" I asked her. I lived vicariously through Valerie's and Meredith's eating.

"Whatever," Meredith said. She was crying. She looked away.

"You look really beautiful, Mer," I said. "You really have that body to beat all." Although Meredith was weary, she looked just great. She had lost about ten pounds on the South Beach Diet, not that she needed to.

"I can't go on," said Meredith.

"You will," I said. "It's Valerie I'm worried about. She's gotta get to the gym." I wanted to reach out for Meredith and hold her and tell her I knew she could get through anything. She'd already been through anything *and* everything. It was kind of odd—as close as we were, my sisters and I never did much touching. Not a lot of hugging and kissing and cradling going on. It was a tradition that had been passed through the chilly bloodlines of our family. As babies and as girls, my sisters and I learned to hold ourselves. We were self-held kids. But you should have seen us with our kids. We shattered the no-hold tradition—and then some. We held our kids whenever we got the chance. I know that if I had gotten healthy, I'd have held them all again. The children would probably have been graduating from high school by that time, but I could see myself picking up my grown nieces and nephews and swinging them around. My sisters wouldn't stand a chance—I'd jump all over them for joy. I'd walk on out to Santa Monica and kiss Reed . . . go twelve rounds with a couple of neurologists I have in mind. I'd never stop moving.

A palpable sadness had settled over the Project A.L.S. camp that Monday, the day before I died. A couple hours after Meredith left the bed for the last time, she called to ask me if I got joy from anything anymore. She said she needed to know. I told her that joy on earth was hard for me to come by recently.

"Does seeing the kids make you happy?" she asked.

"I get joy from seeing them, Mer, but I'm losing my energy to love them in the way that I need to."

"I don't believe that," said Meredith. She didn't believe that the Love Girl was running out of steam. But it took strength to love—really love someone—and in recent days I'd felt that energy changing. Loving on the level that Valerie, Meredith, and I loved throughout our lives takes so much generosity. Loving isn't passive. I think that people feel slighted most of the time. They don't want to give love out to others—they don't want to put out the effort—because they didn't get love themselves. It takes a real effort to turn hurt feelings around. It takes real courage to put your love out there. I longed to put my love on the bed, on this earth, with all of the people I loved in the flesh, but I was being called away. My last conversation with Meredith wasn't our most satisfying. I talked to Meredith about my deteriorating speech, which had made it hard for me to form words like deteriorating. Meredith and I tried to imagine sitting together on the bed not being able to talk to each other. Not being able to shop together, eat together, talk—neither of us could picture it, the not talking. I worried about not being able to take care of her anymore. Who would take my place? Meredith and I said good-bye at around eleven.

I had said good-bye to Valerie the day before, on Sunday. She was in the living room, working on this book. I'd slept all day. She stopped writing at about five to come in and see me. She knocked and slid back the door.

"Hey," she said.

"Hey," I said. "Can you believe how much I sleep?"

"Sleep is a good thing. Sometimes it's the best thing," she said, sitting on the bed. Sleep wasn't the best thing. The best thing was feeling Valerie writing on the other side of my bedroom door. She had worked hard that day. She looked like she could use a break, so we turned on Lifetime. Valerie and I watched a made-for-TV movie starring Meredith Baxter and Swoosie Kurtz until night. We loved TV movies. In this one, Swoosie's daughter was having an affair with the husband of her mother's best friend, played by Meredith Baxter. The husband was so unappealing! Valerie and I couldn't figure out why anyone would want to throw it overboard for him. We talked about our book during commercials.

"I'm so proud of the writing," I said. "I'm so proud of you."

"There's nothing to be proud of," Valerie said. No matter what I said to Valerie lately she couldn't take it in. She was temporarily made of stone—completely unable to absorb a compliment. She seemed determined to stay in this stony state until I got healthy again. She wasn't going to budge until the miracle came, until I got up and danced. I think Valerie saw it as her job to make me better. Until that day came, nothing else would matter. I kept trying to tell Valerie that the celebration was now— our forty years together.

"I love what you've written so far," I said. "You're such a good writer."

"I just listen to your voice on the tapes," she said. "Stop overblowing things."

"Okeydokey," I said as Meredith Baxter hauled off and slapped Swoosie right across the face in a shopping center parking lot. When Swoosie reeled back from the blow and banged into a parked car, Valerie and I laughed until we couldn't breathe. That was maybe about two seconds for me—but you know what I mean. Valerie and I loved acting and actors and movies. All acting; all singing; all dancing—bring it on forever. I remembered when Valerie was going to write movies and I was going to produce and act in them. Valerie, Meredith, and I were going to have our own film production company. That would have been great, I thought, but no greater than this—sitting on the bed with Valerie watching Lifetime.

Here's the thing with this rising: My memories are fueling the ride. My memories are providing the rocket fuel. It turns out I can't go up—unless I go back. The more I see my life as it was, the more I rise. The memories are coming fast and furious: watching Meredith and Peter kiss during our first picnic at West Point; holding two-year-old Willis as he shook with delight after Aldo the horse ate a carrot from his hand; dancing in my apartment on Seventy-first Street before work; braiding Jane's hair; eating a blueberry muffin at my desk at Naked Angels; changing Jake's diaper; getting kisses and kisses from Kate; holding hands with my boyfriend Michael as we walked through the high school breezeway; watching James take his first steps; joking with Scott at the dinner table while Valerie served up chicken and rice; shopping for fake nails at Polk's; taking my bows with the cast of *Men in White,* a play at NYU; eating corn on the cob with Simon in Shelter Island; throwing a clay pot on the kick wheel at Buck's Rock Work Camp; feeling my body against Reed's in the ocean—the ocean, the ocean; running with my sisters as girls in the surf at Playland Beach; wondering in awe at the mystery of my mother's beauty; holding a cup of hot coffee.

I made my own way in life. I had my own style. We all make our own ways and create our own styles. Yes, I wish that I had had more time to hone that style, to tweak it and love it completely just because it was mine, but I didn't. I am thinking and I'm sure, even if life deals us the unimaginable, the absolute ugliest, most intimidating set of circumstances, we can cut a road through it. My sisters and I built a road. We built a road and grew up to be loving, caring, hardworking people, in spite of the odds. My friends and family and I built a road. Project A.L.S. will continue to search until it finds medicine to help people who are dying cruel and inhuman deaths. There are so many roads for us to build that we can and must build. The building is the miracle. As we build, as we work, the ugliest of circumstances will start looking a little less ugly, then less ugly, then they'll look decent bordering on mildly attractive. One day, the road we build will end in a destination. We'll celebrate our fine work together until which time we must go it alone.

I see Meredith now. She's in her kitchen. She is taking a container of sliced cantaloupe out of the refrigerator. She puts the cantaloupe and some bananas on the counter, where Jane and James are sitting and eating breakfast. Jake comes in. He is doing his homework at the last minute. His mother is mad about the homework. She tells him to take a banana. James puts an entire strawberry into his mouth. Here comes Peter, Big Poppa. He's wearing a crisp white shirt for work. He's carrying a tie to put on in the car. He's on the run. The whole family is looking forward to the workmen coming today. Soon the Hulberts will have an addition built on to their house. It will have a playroom, a family room, and a new bedroom for Jake, who is really coming into his own. I have never seen love like this—the yelling and eating and getting ready. After Peter and the kids leave, Meredith will spend the rest of the morning crying on her bed. Then she'll stop crying and take a train into the city. She will buy a large iced tea with one Sweet'n Low and take it up to the office, on Twelfth Street, where she will work for Project A.L.S. until night. Before she goes home on the train, she will drop off her favorite pictures of me at the frame shop. When she gets home she'll tell everyone about the pictures of me that will be coming into the house. Then everyone will go to sleep. Meredith will call Valerie about a hundred times during the day. This is after they've spent the entire day working together at the office.

I see Valerie now. She is almost ready to wrap Christmas presents. She's in my room on Twelfth Street. It's late at night on Christmas Eve. It's one in the morning. Valerie will wrap presents for Willis and Kate at my house because she doesn't want to get caught doing it at her house. Kate believes in Santa Claus. This is probably the last year that Willis will believe, but he still believes. Valerie has come straight from Riverside Memorial Chapel, where she picked up my ashes at about nine o'clock. The man at Riverside gave her a shopping bag with a cherrywood box inside. Valerie took the bag back to the car, lifted the box out of the bag, and put it in the passenger seat. She put the seat belt around the box, then she and I went for one last ride around the city. We drove by the tree at Rockefeller Center, and Naked Angels, which is now a thrift shop, and my old apartment on Seventy-first Street. Valerie wept and drove. She rolled down the windows and screamed at New York. Then she stopped weeping. She parked the car, came up to my place, and put Annie Lennox on my boom box. Now she is starting to wrap. She'll finish in time to surprise Scott and the kids with presents and breakfast in the morning. It's beginning to look a lot like Christmas. Valerie will call Meredith from my phone in the middle of the night. They'll talk. They'll see each other Christmas afternoon. Meredith is making dinner for everyone in Harrison.

We go on. The gentle, three-headed monster Valerie-Jenifer-Meredith will continue to roam the earth. That's what my sisters and I do. We love. We work. We roam. I'm not in the phone loop anymore, but I am here, rising, free, moving, sending love. Everything is going to be okay. There are no boundaries for me now. This is the next world. It is a world of action—rising—and no equal and opposite reaction, at least so far. There is one, unchallenged motion here—up. At the moment, my love is free to rise and seek and stretch out. I like it. It reminds me of the way I felt when I was in the water with Reed, when I felt my love for life stretching out across the infinite ocean.

I don't know what's next for me, if there is a next. If there is, I'd be grateful for a skating rink of some kind. I like this upward motion, but I still have an urge to glide on ice. I could do it now. I could do it again now that I'm free. The ice was always so beautiful in my life. My mother would dress my sisters and me alike in yellow jackets and blue stretch pants; then she'd send us out. As the afternoons wore on, we yellow jackets would meet in the middle of the rink and form a smaller circle of our own. We'd hold on to one another, skating in a circle until the night came. Our yellow jackets were the brightest thing in the dark. When it was closing time at Ebersol Rink, my sisters and I would all just fall down dizzy onto our backs on the ice. I'd look up at the stars and take a deep breath. Oh my, the stars. Oh my. I wanted to touch them and knew that someday, in some way, I would. So here I am. I'd be grateful for a skating rink. I hope there's a snack bar. Meantime, I can say about death what I knew about life: It's not about letting go, but reaching.

Afterword

BY VALERIE ESTESS

M Y GUIDE, the love of my life, my sister Jenifer died on December 16, 2003, then Meredith and I finished this book. Our hearts were shattered but we completed the job. Jenifer always taught me that starting a job was one thing—and admirable—but that following through and completing—well, that's where the bravery is. Ultimately, it didn't matter if the end product was magnificent or mediocre or critically acclaimed. What mattered, Jenifer told me, was the work itself, from beginning to middle to end. So I delivered this manuscript covered with tears to our abiding publishers a couple of weeks ago.

I hope that this book serves up a small inspiring portion of Jenifer's life to you, the reader. Jenifer wasn't wealthy or a supermodel or a pampered pooch. She was a working girl who put on her best face, fought for the life she dreamed of having, and dedicated her last years to fighting the sorry state of brain disease research. Not a shabby résumé. Not her first choice by any stretch, but Jenifer's

205

story shows that sometimes, your Plan B can be okay, better than okay—miraculous. There's gold for us along the way if we can open our eyes enough to see it. The gold is in the getting there, in the holding on, in the reaching. That was Jenifer's experience. Maybe it's yours, too.

Meredith, Project A.L.S., and I continue the fight against ALS and its relatives, Parkinson's, Alzheimer's, and Huntington's diseases. It would be downright un-American of us to quit now. We will keep working from our love for Jenifer and our respect for the millions of adults and children who are being cut down needlessly by these scourges. Project A.L.S. and others are helping scientists approach research in a whole new way. Scientists are working as teammates now—as a dedicated family—so we should be putting effective medicine into place soon.

I always used to whine to Jenifer that the world seemed divided into two groups: the haves and the have-nots. When Jenifer was diagnosed with ALS at the age of thirty-five, I cried that my sisters and I were have-nots. As I railed and stomped my feet, Jenifer just sat on her bed, regal, suggesting that I might want to take a closer look at my own life. As far as Jenifer was concerned, anyone who shared the love that she, Meredith, and I had shared was a have. For Jenifer, having it all was a simple, exquisite recipe, like the one for Kaka's brownies. Combine love, work, compassion, and you will some day, in some way, get to the mountaintop. Making the climb is the ultimate honor and privilege, I now know. I love Jenifer for teaching me that and everything else.

Acknowledgments

My sisters and I acknowledge the extraordinary efforts of Harriet Abramson, Jace Alexander, Jane Alexander, Jennifer Aniston, Debbon Ayer, Hank Azaria, Jon Robin Baitz, William Baldwin, Willow Bay, Vicki and Marc Beckerman, Kathie Berlin, Michael Berman, Cynthia Bernardie, Sara Bernstein, Basilia Billups, David Blaine, Joe Blake, Tessa Blake, Michael Boatman, Michael Bolton, Barry Bostwick, Sofia Bragat, Matthew Broderick, Daniel Brodie, Andrea Brown, Robert H. Brown Jr., Nicole Burdette, Jonathan Burkhart, Rob Burnett, Bobby Canavalle, Nina Capelli, Maureen Carlo, Gail Carson, Tom Cavanaugh, Arnie Civins, Robert Clarke, George Clooney, Lorna Cofield, Maddie Corman, Katie Couric, Sheryl Crow, Carson Daly, Ronnie Davis, Alice and Phillip Decter, Darci DeMatteo, Diana DeRosa, Matt Dillon, Nadine Donahue, Kathi Doolan, Caryle Duffy, Karen Duffy, Paul Eckstein, Ron Eldard, Cornelia Erpf, Alison Estess, Marilyn Estess, Melissa Etheridge, Edie Falco, Gerald D. Fischbach, Steven Fisher, Brenda Friend, Michael J. Fox,

Robert Fumarelli, Fred H. Gage, Matthew Gallagher, James Gandolfini, Janeane Garofalo, Kathleen Gates, John Gearhart, Stephanie George, Gina Gershon, Thomas Gibson, David Marshall Grant, Clark Gregg, Brad Grey, Jill Grey, Harry Grossman, Marlene Haffner, Simon Halls, Lorraine Hamilton, Donna Hanover, Mariska Hargitay, Patricia Harrington, Peter Hedges, Joanna Heimbold, John and Peggy Henry, Juliet Hercules, Gloria and Howard Hirsch, David Hoffenberg, Julianne Hoffenberg, Juliette Hohnen, Joy Huang, Peter J. Hulbert, Bonnie Hunt, Helen Hunt, Kevin Huvane, Robert Iger, Karen Jack, Myra and Allen Jacobson, David L. Jaffe, Andrew Jarecki, Nancy Jarecki, Thomas Jessell, Kristen Johnston, Jane Kaczmarek, Robert S. Kaplan, Brian Kaspar, Carol and Gerald Kaufman, Daniel Kellison, Jimmy Kimmel, Dana and Richard Kind, Greg Kinnear, Linda Kirschenbaum, Jill Knee, Jane Krakowski, Peter Krause, Regina Kulik, Brigitte Lacombe, Jonathan LaPook, Laura Lavelle, Charla Lawhon, Sharon Lawrence, Sue Leibman, Robert Levine, Jaqueline Lividini, Kenneth Lonergan, Bryan Lourd, Joseph Lovett, Richard Lovett, Kyle MacLachlan, Mitchell G. Mandell, Pam Manela and John LaFemina, Camryn Manheim, Julianna Margulies, Jesse L. Martin, Sandy Martin, Michael Mastro, Adam Max, Diane Max, Chi McBride, Martha McCully, Ashley McDermott, Jeffrey McDermott, The McGraths, Valerie McLarty, The Meads, Memory, Jack Merrill, Cori Miller, Dana Miller, Penelope Ann Miller, Katherine Moore, Julie and Rob Moran, Rob Morrow, Geoffrey Nauffts, Sheila Nevins, Fernanda Niven, Philip Noguchi, David O'Connor, Jim Oelschlager,

Cheri Oteri, Pippin Parker, Sarah Jessica Parker, Luke Perry, Brad Pitt, Michael Price, Jason Priestley, Frank Pugliese, Tim Ransom, Dana and Christopher Reeve, Caroline Rhea, Ron Rifkin, Scott Robbins, Janine Rose, Jeffrey D. Rothstein, Lewis P. Rowland, Alan Ruck, Paul Rudd, Reed Rudy, Dale Ryan, Laura SanGiacomo, Richard Santulli, Lou Saporito, Kim Schefler-Rodriguez, Annabella Sciorra, Frederic Seegal, Molly Shannon, Edward Sherin, Brooke Shields, Linda G. Singer, Evan Snyder, Vincent Spano, Fisher Stevens, Jon Stewart, Ben Stiller, Michael Sweedler, D. B. Sweeney, Pamela and Laurence Tarica, Jamie Tarses, Christine Taylor, Carol Thompson, Maura Tierney, Marisa Tomei, Nancy Travis, Blair Underwood, Asnal Valcin, Jamie Walsh, Jennifer Ward, Juliet Weber, Steven Weber, Marion Weil, Titus Welliver, Tom Werner, Linda and the Wertliebs, Bradley White, Debbie Wilpon, Fred Wilpon, Richard Wilpon, Cyd Wilson, Scott Wolf, Richard Wood, and the thousands across the country who have given so generously of their time and efforts on behalf of finding a cure.

I especially wish to recognize Judith Curr for her vision, and my editor, Tracy Behar, for her singular guidance in writing this book.